W9-BVD-604

THE IMPORTANCE OF

Jonas Salk

Jonas Salk

These and other titles are included in The Importance Of biography series:

Maya Angelou
Louis Armstrong
James Baldwin
Lucille Ball
The Beatles
Alexander Graham Bell
Napoleon Bonaparte
Julius Caesar
Rachel Carson
Charlie Chaplin
Charlemagne
Winston Churchill
Christopher Columbus
Leonardo da Vinci
James Dean
Charles Dickens
Walt Disney
Dr. Seuss
F. Scott Fitzgerald
Anne Frank
Benjamin Franklin
Mohandas Gandhi
John Glenn
Jane Goodall

Martha Graham
Lorraine Hansberry
Ernest Hemingway
Adolf Hitler
Thomas Jefferson
John F. Kennedy
Martin Luther King Jr.
Bruce Lee
John Lennon
Douglas MacArthur
Margaret Mead
Golda Meir
Mother Teresa
John Muir
Richard M. Nixon
Pablo Picasso
Edgar Allan Poe
Queen Elizabeth I
Jonas Salk
Margaret Sanger
William Shakespeare
Frank Sinatra
Tecumseh
Simon Wiesenthal

THE IMPORTANCE OF

Jonas Salk

by James Barter

LUCENT BOOKS
SAN DIEGO, CALIFORNIA

THOMSON

GALE

Detroit • New York • San Diego • San Francisco
Boston • New Haven, Conn. • Waterville, Maine
London • Munich

Library of Congress Cataloging-in-Publication Data

Barter, James, 1946–
    Jonas Salk / by James Barter.
        p. cm. — (The importance of)
Includes bibliographical references and index.
    ISBN 1-56006-968-6 (hbk. : alk. paper)
    1. Salk, Jonas, 1914– —Juvenile literature. 2. Virologists—
United States—Biography—Juvenile literature. 3. Poliomyelitis
vaccine—Juvenile literature. 4. Poliomyelitis—Vaccination—
Juvenile literature. [1. Salk, Jonas, 1914– 2. Scientists.
3. Poliomyelitis vaccine.] I. Title. II. Series.
    QR31.S25 B374 2003
    610'.92—dc21

2001006050

Copyright 2002 by Lucent Books,
an imprint of The Gale Group
10911 Technology Place, San Diego, California 92127

Printed in the U.S.A.

Contents

Foreword

THE IMPORTANCE OF biography series deals with individuals who have made a unique contribution to history. The editors of the series have deliberately chosen to cast a wide net and include people from all fields of endeavor. Individuals from politics, music, art, literature, philosophy, science, sports, and religion are all represented. In addition, the editors did not restrict the series to individuals whose accomplishments have helped change the course of history. Of necessity, this criterion would have eliminated many whose contribution was great, though limited. Charles Darwin, for example, was responsible for radically altering the scientific view of the natural history of the world. His achievements continue to impact the study of science today. Others, such as Chief Joseph of the Nez Percé, played a pivotal role in the history of their own people. While Joseph's influence does not extend much beyond the Nez Percé, his nonviolent resistance to white expansion and his continuing role in protecting his tribe and his homeland remain an inspiration to all.

These biographies are more than factual chronicles. Each volume attempts to emphasize an individual's contributions both in his or her own time and for posterity. For example, the voyages of Christopher Columbus opened the way to European colonization of the New World. Unquestionably, his encounter with the New World brought monumental changes to both Europe and the Americas in his day. Today, however, the broader impact of Columbus's voyages is being critically scrutinized. *Christopher Columbus*, as well as every biography in The Importance Of series, includes and evaluates the most recent scholarship available on each subject.

Each author includes a wide variety of primary and secondary source quotations to document and substantiate his or her work. All quotes are footnoted to show readers exactly how and where biographers derive their information, as well as provide stepping stones to further research. These quotations enliven the text by giving readers eyewitness views of the life and times of each individual covered in The Importance Of series.

Finally, each volume is enhanced by photographs, bibliographies, chronologies, and comprehensive indexes. For both the casual reader and the student engaged in research, The Importance Of biographies will be a fascinating adventure into the lives of people who have helped shape humanity's past and present, and who will continue to shape its future.

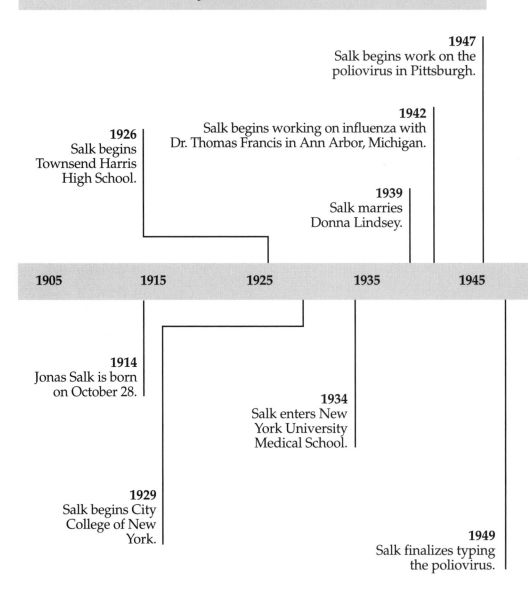

IMPORTANT DATES IN THE LIFE OF JONAS SALK

1947
Salk begins work on the poliovirus in Pittsburgh.

1942
Salk begins working on influenza with Dr. Thomas Francis in Ann Arbor, Michigan.

1926
Salk begins Townsend Harris High School.

1939
Salk marries Donna Lindsey.

| 1905 | 1915 | 1925 | 1935 | 1945 |

1914
Jonas Salk is born on October 28.

1934
Salk enters New York University Medical School.

1929
Salk begins City College of New York.

1949
Salk finalizes typing the poliovirus.

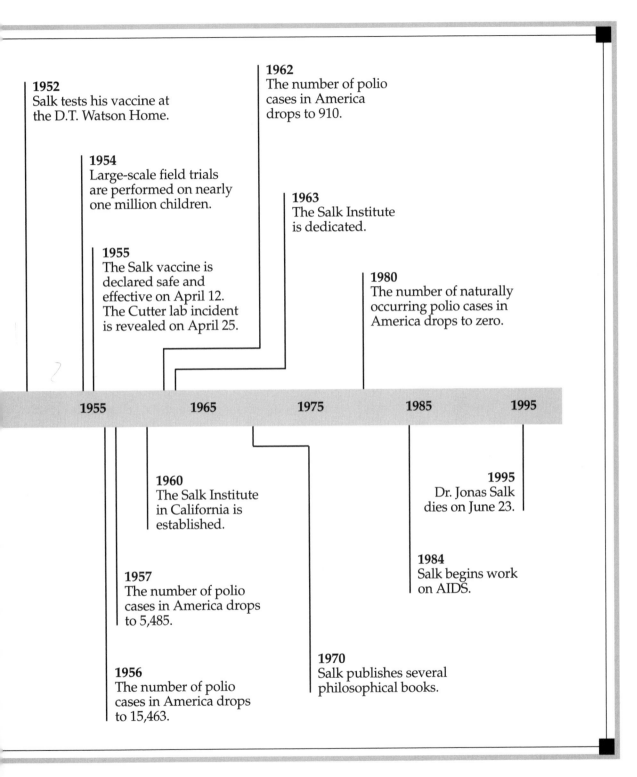

1952
Salk tests his vaccine at the D.T. Watson Home.

1962
The number of polio cases in America drops to 910.

1954
Large-scale field trials are performed on nearly one million children.

1963
The Salk Institute is dedicated.

1955
The Salk vaccine is declared safe and effective on April 12. The Cutter lab incident is revealed on April 25.

1980
The number of naturally occurring polio cases in America drops to zero.

1955   1965   1975   1985   1995

1960
The Salk Institute in California is established.

1995
Dr. Jonas Salk dies on June 23.

1957
The number of polio cases in America drops to 5,485.

1984
Salk begins work on AIDS.

1970
Salk publishes several philosophical books.

1956
The number of polio cases in America drops to 15,463.

The Forgotten Epidemic

During the spring of 1955, millions of children rambled home from elementary school with permission slips to be given to their parents and returned signed the next day. To the casual glance of the children, the white slips they had pinned to their sweaters, tucked into spelling books, and stuffed in lunch boxes appeared to be just like the others they often were given for field trips, bus passes, school pictures, after-school sports, and parent-teacher conferences.

When the parents unfolded the wrinkled bits of paper and began reading them, however, their reactions were anything but casual. They eagerly signed the slips permitting their children to be inoculated with a new vaccine, developed by Dr. Jonas Salk. They hoped this new vaccine would protect their children against the crippling and often deadly disease called poliomyelitis.

This disease, commonly called polio, struck randomly, and its victims were primarily children. For decades parents had been hoping for a vaccine that would end this tragic suffering. America suffered the worst outbreak of polio in 1952 when 57,740 new cases were reported. By 1955 nearly everyone had a family member, a relative, or a neighborhood friend who walked on crutches or had their legs clamped into metal braces because of this crippling disease. Polio attacks the central nervous system, causing paralysis and, in severe cases, death.

The inoculations of the Salk vaccine that each child received in 1955 ended the spread of this dreaded childhood disease. Within a handful of years there were no new polio victims who would need wood crutches, metal leg braces, child-sized wheelchairs, and iron lungs—machines that encased patients' bodies to help them breathe.

By the mid-1960s new cases of polio had nearly vanished from America. The chance of contracting the disease had fallen below that of being struck by lightning. As quickly as the feared disease once struck down children, it just as quickly disappeared. Best of all, the public no longer heard the horrifying stories about polio epidemics and parents no longer lived in fear of waking their children in the morning for school to hear the dreaded words, "Mom, I can't move my legs."

The public never understood how the vaccine worked nor how it was made, and few probably cared. What they cared about was that the epidemic had ended and that

Dr. Jonas Salk deserved to be honored as a national hero—and he was.

At the beginning of the twenty-first century, those who were alive fifty years before and were lucky to escape polio no longer talk about the disease, although the name Dr. Salk still rings with a heroic tone. As for younger Americans, few under forty have had any experience with polio and even fewer under thirty recognize the word "polio" or the name Dr. Salk. These simple facts, which illustrate the disappearance of polio from America's list of health concerns, are two of the greatest compliments that can be paid to Dr. Salk.

Another compliment worthy of Dr. Salk's great achievement is keeping the story of Dr. Salk alive. His story is about more than the discovery of the polio vaccine, although that would occupy the central chapters of his life. There are many earlier chapters detailing his education, commitment to hard work, brilliant medical observations, and self-sacrifice. And following the discovery there are many chapters depicting both the glitter and the

A Baltimore doctor injects a schoolgirl with Jonas Salk's polio vaccine in 1955.

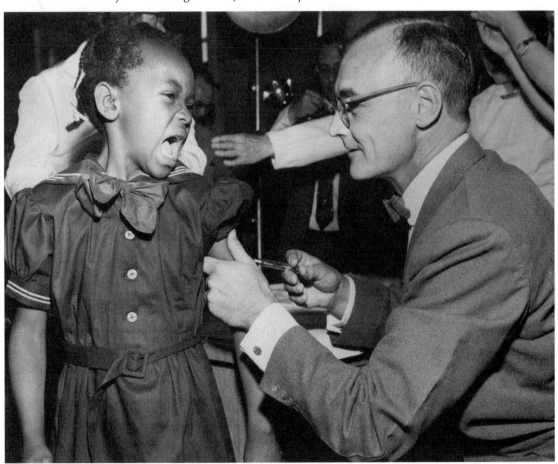

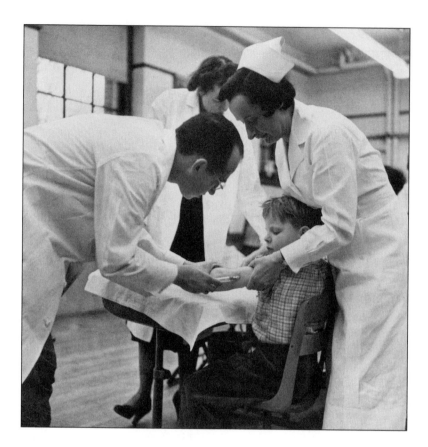

A boy receives a polio inoculation. Salk's vaccine ended the polio epidemic in the United States.

dark side of fame, Salk's continuing struggles to find new medical breakthroughs, and his efforts to find solutions to some of the world's most pressing problems.

There are many valuable lessons to be learned from studying Dr. Salk's rich and unconventional life. As writer Bob Green said, "In an age when the term 'hero' is used to apply to everyone from rock singers to soap opera stars, Dr. Jonas Salk may be the most genuine hero we have. None of us should ever forget why this is so."[1]

1 Preparing for Success

Great scientific discoveries do not usually occur by accident. They are rare events, and when they occur, the world pauses to bestow recognition on those people who discovered them. All notable scientists who have stood at the apex of a great triumph have arrived there because they have prepared themselves to achieve success. Dr. Jonas Salk was no exception.

Salk, like other exceptional scientific minds, points to his early years as being the most significant training period for his later work. According to some psychologists, it is in these early years that a person's character develops and becomes the foundation on which the rest of his or her life will be constructed. For Jonas Salk, these were the years he developed his quest for new ideas, his drive for perfection, and a work ethic that allowed him to focus his efforts on achieving success.

COMING TO AMERICA

Even before Jonas Salk's birth, his future was being planned for him by his parents, Daniel and Dora Salk. Dora had come to America

Hungry Russians line up to receive food aid. At the turn of the twentieth century, many Russians, Salk's mother included, fled famine and poverty in their homeland for a better life in America.

from Russia in 1901, thirteen years before Jonas's birth, to escape the anti-Semitism, devastating poverty, and violence under the Russian autocratic ruling family, the Romanovs. Dora was one of tens of thousands of people who risked all that they had to find a new home that could provide better opportunities for them and their children. America appealed to many immigrants because at the turn of the twentieth century, it was still a relatively new nation that was beginning to dominate world events and world finances.

Arriving in America with little money and no job, twelve-year-old Dora soon began working in a garment factory in New York's garment district. Eventually, she met and married Daniel, a native of New Jersey. Daniel also worked in the garment district, which is where most of the nation's clothes were designed and manufactured. The couple moved into an apartment in the West Bronx, a poor neighborhood located on the northern end of Manhattan Island in New York City, and began their family.

On October 28, 1914, Dora gave birth to Jonas, the first of the Salks' three children. Growing up, he spent most of his time with his mother, who had stopped working after she married. As Jonas grew, his parents recognized that he had a quick mind. Jonas seemed interested in everything around him and enjoyed collecting information to share with others. Jonas passed much of his time by himself inside the family's apartment. There he became accustomed to the chattering of his neighbors and the smells of cooking in the hallways of their apartment building.

DORA SALK

Dora was the driving force in Jonas's early life. She was an extremely attentive mother to Jonas and attacked the job of raising him with great zeal, viewing this responsibility as her destiny. Richard Carter, Jonas Salk's biographer, said of her passion for raising Jonas, "She designed him for fame. She felt it her duty to make her presence felt in the world through her sons."[2]

Dora taught Jonas how to become a successful problem solver. A strong-willed woman, she set exceptionally high standards for young Jonas. Eager to please his mother, he responded positively each time that she imposed increasingly higher standards. For example, she would give him simple tasks to perform such as building a house with wood blocks. When he succeeded, she would reward him and then have him build another, more complicated one. As Dora continued to raise her expectations for Jonas, he happily and diligently applied himself to meet them. As a result, he learned the valuable lesson that he could successfully solve just about any problem handed to him. Dora carried out this cycle of success followed by reward in many of his playtime activities.

Dora was determined to prepare Jonas for success. Her experience first with the violence of Russia and then in the poverty of New York instilled in Dora the belief that childhood was a testing ground that would later determine who would achieve success in life and who would not. Jonas never forgot what it was like growing up poor in New York, and later in his life he attributed his forceful personality to his early experience with poverty as a child. He observed that as a person who has very little and wants something, "you overcome the resistances to any opposition."[3]

Dora was not satisfied to allow her children to run loose in the streets without supervision and without some constructive purpose. She did not believe that success would come to those spending their time playing stickball in the streets of New York, running across the rooftops, or chasing each other up and down the black iron fire-escape ladders attached to the exteriors of the old apartment houses.

Success, Dora believed, would come to those who worked for it. She taught her sons how to succeed for several reasons, but none more important than her belief that one day it would lead them to jobs and in-

As a child, Salk lived with his family in a poor section of New York City called the West Bronx (pictured).

come that would allow them to escape the poverty of their neighborhood in the Bronx. She expected her sons to improve their lives. Jonas Salk remembered his mother's commitment to her children in a 1991 interview:

> She wanted her children to have more than she had, so that she lived her life, and invested her life through her children. I was the eldest of three sons and the favorite and the one who had all of her attention, certainly until my little brother was born—I was about five years old then—and my youngest brother when I was about twelve. I was essentially an only child in the sense of having her interest and concerns and attention. She wanted to be sure that we all were going to advance in the world. Therefore we were encouraged in our studies, and overly protected in many ways.[4]

ENCOURAGING A CURIOUS MIND

As Jonas's young personality began to develop, Dora began to consider what other qualities he would need to succeed in America. She had already begun to foster in Jonas an appreciation for hard work in whatever tasks he might undertake and for doing them well. She also believed that stimulating his curiosity was crucial for developing an interest in learning about the world.

Jonas had a natural sense of curiosity that would play a major role in his later success as a scientist. As Salk commented later in his life:

I think I was curious from the earliest age on. There was a photograph of me and there was that look of curiosity on that infant's face that is inescapable. I have the suspicion that this curiosity was very much a part of my early life: asking questions about unreasonableness. I tended to observe, and reflect and wonder. [5]

Dora also encouraged Jonas's curiosity by using precious household money to provide for him books or materials that caught his interest. As a boy, Jonas enjoyed reading about great scientists, explorers, and historical leaders. In this regard, Jonas later recognized that his parents had created a unique environment for him and his brothers: "There was something special in the household, that was very nurturing for, shall we say, advancing in the world, getting ahead. But whether it was in business or in law or in medicine, so to speak, was not of great concern." [6]

For Dora, nurturing Jonas's curiosity knew no bounds. For her Jewish family, she maintained a kosher house, which meant, among other things, that pork was not permitted. One day when Jonas was older and in medical school, he was required to measure his blood chemistry before eating a fatty meat that included bacon. Dora was opposed to allowing the pork into her kosher house; however, because it was an educational experiment, she allowed Jonas to proceed. To separate the educational requirement, which she respected, from the religious rules of her house, which she also respected, she bought Jonas a frying pan that she afterward threw away. And during the frying of the bacon, she locked herself in a bedroom to avoid the smell.

THE DESIRE TO EXCEL

Dora and Daniel did not push Jonas in any particular direction, but they did expect him to excel in everything that he attempted. When Jonas was just twelve years old, his ability to excel was put to the test. His parents took him to apply to Townsend Harris High School, which catered to unusually bright, promising students who could demonstrate their exceptional academic talents. The school counselors tested Jonas. Based on the examination results, the school accepted him although he was much younger than most of the other freshmen. Townsend Harris had a reputation for demanding exceptionally high-quality work and commitment from its students or they were removed from the school. The school could do this because it provided the best academic program available within the New York City public school system, and it was free to all who qualified. In addition to its high academic standards, the school also required each student to complete the usual four-year high school academic program in just three years.

Although Jonas was younger than most of his freshmen classmates, Dora had prepared him to succeed. Jonas thrived among the exceptionally bright and motivated students in his classes. The persistent work ethic, curiosity, and value of perfection that his mother had taught him paved a successful academic road during his three years at Townsend Harris. Eager to learn and even more eager to meet each new challenge, Jonas prepared for his exams and wrote his research papers by thoroughly immersing

At Townsend Harris High School, Salk (pictured here as an adult) was a successful, ambitious student.

himself in all his subjects. One of Jonas's teachers remembered him as a boy "who read everything that he could lay his hands on."[7]

Jonas's enthusiasm for perfection extended to everything he did. Many years later, when asked by his wife to clean the stove, he spent three hours cleaning every corner, front and back. He finished the job using toothpicks to clean the slots of the screws holding the stove together.

EARLY AMBITION

While at Townsend Harris, Jonas's academic success gave him the confidence to begin thinking about his future. During those three years he began to develop a very ambitious general life plan that he would often refer to in his adult life as his guiding light. The plan was that "Someday I shall grow up and do something in my own way, without anyone telling me how."[8]

Although the idea of doing something in his own way was a very general ambition, he had others that were more specific. Pursuing a medical career had not yet occurred to him, but he knew that he wanted a professional career. He admired his father and mother for their long hours of hard physical work, but he wanted to help more people in a bigger way—he dreamed of studying law and becoming a congressman.

Days before Salk's fifteenth birthday in 1929, he graduated from Townsend Harris High School and began his college career at City College of New York with a surge of confidence in himself and his future: "I knew I was competent, I knew I had proved it by achieving that which I was supposed to achieve, time and time again. The remainder of childhood was for me a period of patient waiting, and not much else."[9]

City College of New York celebrates its 75th anniversary in 1922. Seven years later, fifteen-year-old Jonas Salk enrolled at the college.

FINDING AN INTEREST TO FIT HIS PERSONALITY

Salk's personality had been largely defined by the time he started college. His mother's insistence that he avoid outdoor play in favor of indoor cultural and intellectual activities sculpted a quiet, introspective personality. Salk's initial interest in pursuing a legal education in college faded as he began taking courses in the sciences. Townsend Harris High School had offered only one science course, physics. As Salk began to discover

other science classes in college, his interest moved in that direction.

Salk became especially interested in chemistry. He found that studying the laws governing chemistry suited his personality more closely than any other subject. He especially enjoyed the logic needed to understand chemistry, and his quiet, introspective nature was a perfect fit for laboratory work. He once recalled:

> I could spend time by myself and I still do. The capacity to spend time alone

was something that I look back upon as having, perhaps, contributed to this kind of introspection. I would say that I spent more time alone than I did in social settings. Part of this was probably attributed to my mother's overprotectiveness, lest I hurt myself, or be injured in some way. . . . Nevertheless, I did learn in time that I did and could spend time alone, as I do, walking on the beach. I spend time with others, of course, but also enjoy time with myself.[10]

Salk approached chemistry with a single-mindedness that he would continue to apply all his life. He worked tirelessly in the chemistry laboratory and eventually developed a reputation for being a "lab rat." Chemistry provided an outlet for Salk's curiosity about the world, and its complexity provided him with the joy of solving problems too difficult for most of his classmates. Working in the laboratory satisfied his need to work independently, and his drive for perfection gave him a reputation as the most promising young chemist in his class.

Salk got along well with his classmates, but he was by no means an outgoing person. He did not particularly enjoy spending idle time with people. A student colleague of his observed, "He was awfully difficult to get to know well. Not that he wasn't agreeable and companionable, but he hoarded his being more than most people do, as if he had walled it up for safekeeping in a sanctuary surrounded by a labyrinth and moats."[11]

In 1934 at the age of nineteen Salk received his bachelor of science degree from City College of New York. He had loved the sciences and had thought a lot about what his next step would be toward determining his life's work.

HELPING HUMANITY

Jonas felt a need to contribute to humanity in some way. He had grown up with an awareness of the suffering of people living in poverty in his neighborhood, and he had heard stories of anti-Semitism and hardship in eastern Europe. He wanted to be able to do something to help his neighbors. Salk once described his first awareness of humanitarian feelings in an interview with journalist Bill Moyers. He was three-and-a-half years old: "I remember seeing troops coming back on Armistice Day in 1918. I recall even as a young child being perplexed by seeing wounded soldiers in the parade."[12] Salk recalled wanting to help the struggling men.

This early desire to help people in need gradually shaped a humanitarian spirit that would be a recurring theme throughout his life. Several years after Salk's death, a colleague and friend, Dr. Walter Eckhart of the Salk Institute, remarked, "Jonas was a great humanitarian. He loved children. He had a strong sense of obligation for future generations. He liked to say, 'We should strive to be good ancestors.'"[13]

Salk graduated from college in 1934. At the time the United States was experiencing one of the decade's worst outbreaks of polio. It crippled thousands of children and even killed many of them. This viral disease attacks the central nervous system causing paralysis most often in the arms or legs, but

President Roosevelt and Polio

No single person brought polio to the attention of the American public more than its most famous victim, President Franklin D. Roosevelt. The only president to suffer from a major debilitating disease, Roosevelt contracted polio in 1921 when he was thirty-nine years old.

One day he was helping to fight a forest fire after taking a swim in the Atlantic Ocean. When he returned home he felt a slight chill and he went to bed. When he awakened the next morning, his right knee felt weak. That evening his knee collapsed while he was walking—he never walked normally again.

Although the public knew the president had polio, his political life was carefully co-ordinated so the public would not see the leg brace he wore or the wheelchair he rode in. When he was photographed, he was shown sitting behind a desk, in a car, or leaning against a railing as he delivered a speech. To disguise his disability as much as possible, the president even had his crutches painted to match his pants and socks.

In 1937, as more and more people, especially small children, contracted the paralyzing disease, Basil O'Connor urged Roosevelt to organize and support the National Foundation for Infantile Paralysis (NFIP). The NFIP would grow over time to become

the leading fund-raising organization in the United States for the fight against polio. Roosevelt held elegant parties at the White House to raise money for the NFIP and went on the radio soliciting all Americans to donate money to the organization. Without the millions of dollars that came from Roosevelt's fund-raising efforts, the successful vaccines of Salk and Sabin would have taken much longer to develop.

America's most famous polio survivor, President Franklin D. Roosevelt.

sometimes in the muscles that control breathing. Those suffering from paralysis of the legs were either confined to wheelchairs or walked with leg braces and crutches. Worse off were the children whose breathing muscles were affected because they had to live in iron lungs that mechanically helped them breathe. Eventually many died. At that time no one knew what caused polio or how it was transmitted. People were terrified of this disease that could strike anyone without warning.

Salk was especially moved by the widespread suffering of small children. The nation's attention was also drawn to the disease because the president of the United States, Franklin Delano Roosevelt, had contracted polio, which had left his legs paralyzed. Consequently, the president was forced to spend the rest of his life in a wheelchair or use braces or crutches to stand or walk.

Against the backdrop of the Great Depression, war looming in Europe, and growing fears of polio, Salk "went through some soul searching,"[14] as he described it. He recognized that his interest in science and his commitment to humanitarian needs pointed toward a career in medicine. In the fall of 1934, he entered the New York University School of Medicine.

Choosing Medical Research

Salk truly believed that he had finally found the profession for which he had been preparing. As each new medical student entered the school, faculty advisers asked in what area of medicine each intended to specialize. Knowing that he could save the lives of thousands if he could find a cure for a widespread disease, Salk declared his area of interest to be medical research rather than a standard medical practice. Salk's adviser admonished him, saying that there was very little money to be made in research. Salk's concern for humanity was evident in his reply, "There is more in life than money."[15]

As a first-year medical student, Salk set himself to meet the challenges of learning as he had done so many times before—with thorough and tireless research until he had perfected his understanding. By the end of Salk's first year, his outstanding work and the passion he applied to it caught the attention of Dr. R. Keith Cannan, who suggested that the prodigious young man might profit from taking a year's leave of absence from the university to study biochemistry exclusively. It was agreed between the two men that Salk would return to medical school the following year to continue his studies.

Salk seized the opportunity and spent the year pursuing a mix of chemistry and medicine that he found very satisfying. He was assigned to work on a particular strain of the streptococcus bacteria that often causes severe throat infections leading to strep throat, scarlet fever, and some forms of pneumonia. Purifying the streptococcus bacteria for research purposes was a painfully slow process. Salk set to work to find a faster and more efficient way to concentrate the bacteria. By the end of the year, he had successfully developed a process using calcium phosphate. He later submitted his results to a medical journal for his first professional publication.

THE IRON LUNG

Polio can affect different parts of the nervous system. One form of polio causes paralysis of the muscles that enable people to breathe. Death followed quickly until the invention of a machine called the iron lung, which breathed for the person artificially.

Technically named a Drinker-Colins respirator after the two men who developed it, the iron lung was an airtight steel tube inside of which the patient's entire body, except for the head, was enclosed. The machine had leather bellows that would expand, causing the pressure inside the iron lung to drop. This caused the patient's chest to expand, forcing air into the lungs through the mouth. When the bellows contracted, the air was forced out.

Thousands of patients lived in warehouse-like rooms in hospitals unable to do little more than lie in iron lungs twenty-four hours a day. Without any physical activity, patients experienced profound boredom. Most eventually died from the paralysis, although some regained use of their breathing muscles. Remarkably, it is estimated that 125 people still are living in iron lungs today. One such person is Mark O'Brien.

O'Brien contracted polio in 1955 when he was six years old. In 1994 he was accepted into an experimental program for quadriplegics at the University of California. When engineers at the university discovered that he could move his left foot, they built him a motorized iron lung that he could operate with foot controls. For the first time in his life he was able to drive himself down hallways and sidewalks and could cross streets with the assistance of mirrors.

On August 21, 1994, O'Brien was interviewed by Daniel Zwerlding of National Public Radio. O'Brien spoke about the moment he arrived at the hospital in 1955: "My parents called the family doctor and then, I don't know, they conferred—all the grown-ups conferred. I was taken to Children's Hospital in downtown Boston. The thing I do remember is they told me to roll over from a gurney onto a bed, and I did that. That was the last thing I did. I mean, I could wiggle my eyebrows and stuff, but that was my last unconscious, whole body movement."

Salk thrived in medical school. After returning to his medical school classes, Salk continued to pursue his interest in research by volunteering to work in the laboratory of Dr. Thomas Francis, a respected microbiologist. During his third year, Salk took time off from his studies to visit a social worker named Donna Lindsey, whom he had met in Woods Hole, Massachusetts, while working summers to earn money. She was a very bright graduate of Smith College who earned admission to the prestigious academic honor society, Phi Beta Kappa. She also shared Jonas's sense of sorrow whenever she saw people suffering. The two began to date, and the day following Jonas's graduation in June 1939, they married. They moved into a New York City apartment on Jonas's salary of $100 a month as a medical researcher at the Rockefeller Institute.

Salk was now in position to move forward with his career in medical research. The qualities for success that he had acquired from his mother during his childhood and his experience in medical school had delivered him to the next great plateau in his life.

2 Becoming a Scientist

Completing medical school had proven nothing more than that Salk had the potential to be a good scientist. Now at the age of twenty-six, he had entered the real world of medical research and he would need to learn an additional set of skills.

Now was the time for Salk to learn the value of psychological skills and diplomacy. While working as an intern in a hospital and as a scientist in a laboratory, Salk learned that becoming accomplished would require him to interact with patients and other doctors, all of whom had differing backgrounds and ideas. Such differences could often lead to conflict and animosity, which if not resolved satisfactorily might become an impediment to good laboratory research.

Salk now also would learn the value and difficulties of challenging orthodox or conventional medical ideas. He recognized that many medical ideas did not hold up to scientific scrutiny. Salk's willingness to question orthodox beliefs provided him with an unusual perspective that prepared him to see solutions missed by others. Salk's scientific curiosity and powers of observation led him to find early success as a young researcher by making discoveries others had not considered possible.

DEVELOPING A HUMAN FACE

In 1940 Salk began a two-year medical internship, which was required of all newly graduated medical students. Every young doctor in New York dreamed of interning at New York's prestigious Mount Sinai hospital, but few were either bright enough or focused enough to qualify. Because of its outstanding reputation, only the top 250 new doctors in New York applied in 1940, and of those, only twelve were taken, one of whom was Salk.

The first attribute that Salk developed as a new doctor was the ability to befriend others. Although he had been a relatively reclusive young student in high school and college, such isolation would be of limited value as a doctor. Salk quickly learned that he would need to develop a human face to complement his intellect.

Salk thrived in the hospital atmosphere, and for the first time in his life, he spent time getting to know the other interns and learning the value of camaraderie. His well-established work ethic of long hours, careful review of all data about diseases, and his demand for perfection earned him the reputation as the most promising of the interns. His fellow interns elected him president of the house staff. Salk recognized this as a step forward in his young career. As president, he would be the interns' representative before the permanent medical staff. Regarding Salk's reputation at the hospital, a senior-level doctor who worked with the young intern said this about him:

> From 1940 to '42 the most stable young man in that place was Jonas Salk. With all the tensions and pressures, the need to learn the arts of medicine, the squabbles about hours and pay and work rules, the excitement about war and politics, and the need to put the patient's interests ahead of everything else, not many interns, residents, or members of the upper crust were able to maintain calm at all times. Furthermore, . . . he was the best damn talker

in the bunch and had the most common sense and most charm.[16]

Salk also began to apply his humanitarian views firsthand when working directly with hospital patients. As an intern, Salk spent time treating all kinds of patients, even though work in the laboratories was his preference. Salk took the time to meet and talk with patients, and in doing so, he learned to share the profound suffering and sense of helplessness that so many of them experienced. As author Jane Smith explains:

> Most polio patients were jammed together in open wards . . . with no regard for age or severity of their case. An infant in an iron lung would be put next to a teenager with a paralyzed

While a resident at New York's Mount Sinai hospital, Salk met many children encased in iron lungs like these. Saddened by the children's suffering, he became interested in developing a cure for polio.

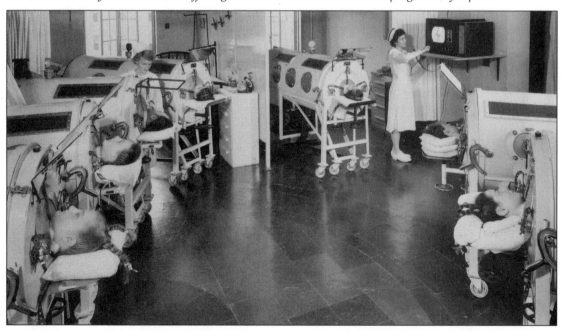

arm, and beyond him lay a distraught postman wondering how he could support his family when he couldn't stand up. [17]

Salk was particularly moved by the suffering of children. At that time most large hospitals had warehouse-like rooms packed with small children encased in barrel-shaped respirators called iron lungs. When Salk walked through the wards talking with the children he wanted to improve their situations. He could do little to help, however, except to talk to them and relieve their pain. Recognizing the tragedy that had overcome their lives, he realized he wanted to begin research on one of the many deadly diseases affecting the world's population.

To Salk, laboratory research might allow him someday to find a cure for polio that would benefit all of humankind, unlike a standard medical practice where his work might benefit only a few. Salk remembered his decision to pursue laboratory work this way, "I believe that this [polio research] is all linked to my original ambition, or desire, which was to be of some help to humankind, so to speak, in a larger sense than just on a one-to-one basis." [18]

QUESTIONING CONVENTIONAL IDEAS

As Salk was mastering his newly discovered social skills, he also began to recognize that he could not accept everything that the faculty was teaching him. As Salk made his rounds in the hospital under the direction of different teaching doctors, he grew suspicious that many senior-level doctors believed and taught theories of medicine without giving them much thought.

Many great thinkers are able to point to a single moment or incident in their lives that proved to be central to their ultimate success, and in this regard Salk was no exception. During a lecture at medical school Salk heard a conventional theory on vaccinations that did not seem logical to him. He began to question the very basis of the theory.

The lecture conveyed the widely held theory that any successful immunization—an inoculation to stimulate resistance—against a viral disease required a vaccine containing small amounts of the infectious live virus itself. Virologists understood that a weakened virus could trigger a person's immune system to defend against the virus without overwhelming and killing the person. Yet Salk had heard in a lecture just the day before that a vaccine made from noninfectious material from the deadly diphtheria and tetanus bacteria could protect against those diseases.

When Salk asked the lecturing doctor about the apparent inconsistency regarding the use of living viruses and nonliving material, the noted lecturer brushed aside his question without a reasonable explanation. Salk remained quiet, yet as a young man who had focused his life on the pursuit of information and on the use of logic, the apparent inconsistency remained in the back of his mind. Much later in life, an interviewer asked Salk when he first challenged conventional wisdom in science, and he answered with this reference to that lecture:

How Vaccines Stimulate the Immune System

The immune system of the body is an extraordinarily complex network of organs, cells, and molecules that act together to protect the body from harmful invading diseases. When a vaccine such as the Salk or Sabin polio vaccine enters a person's body, for example, the virus contained in the vaccine, commonly called an antigen, stimulates the immune system into action.

As the antigen courses through the blood, several components of the immune system detect it. During this first exposure to the antigen, called the primary response, several days pass before the immune system becomes fully activated. During this period, specific types of white blood cells called lymphocytes are produced in the bone marrow, and they locate and surround the invading antigen and "map" the characteristics of its surface.

During the next phase, the lymphocytes that have mapped the surface of the antigen produce large concentrations of antibodies, which are protein molecules carried in the blood. They search out the antigen based on the mapping information, and kill it. After the antibodies successfully fend off the attack, the antibody concentration declines.

During the next phase, the immune system activates the production of a different type of lymphocyte that acts as a memory cell. These lymphocytes "memorize" the mapping of the antigen so that if that particular virus should return in the future, the immune system will quickly trigger a secondary response. During this response antibodies are produced much faster than the first time the immune system encountered the antigen. This process of memorizing the mapping of an antigen is called immunological memory. These "memory cells" will usually remain in the bloodstream for the remainder of a person's life.

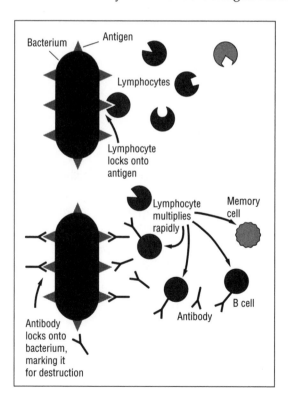

Bacterium — Antigen
Lymphocytes
Lymphocyte locks onto antigen
Lymphocyte multiplies rapidly
Memory cell
B cell
Antibody
Antibody locks onto bacterium, marking it for destruction

We were told in one lecture that it was possible to immunize against diphtheria and tetanus by the use of chemically treated toxins, or toxoids. And the following lecture, we were told that for immunization against a virus disease, you have to experience the infection, and that you could not induce immunity with the so-called "killed" or inactivated, chemically treated virus preparation. Well, somehow, that struck me. What struck me was that both statements couldn't be true. And I asked why this was so, and the answer that was given was in a sense, "Because." There was no satisfactory answer. [19]

Salk felt that the issue about the live versus the killed viruses was in need of further investigation. "I just didn't accept what appeared to me to be a dogmatic assertion in view of the fact that there was a reason to think otherwise. So that it was not merely doubting a belief, there was a principle that was involved." [20] Salk would later return to this debate, which would become the central piece of the puzzle that led to the development of the first successful polio vaccine.

Salk completed his intership before he could resolve this apparent contradiction. In need of a job as a research scientist, Salk sent out his résumé to several universities and research institutes and awaited a good offer to begin his professional career.

EARLY SUCCESS

Salk did not have to wait long for an employment offer. Dr. Thomas Francis, who had met and been impressed by Salk in medical school, invited him to perform research at the University of Michigan at Ann Arbor. Francis recognized Salk's capabilities as well as his ambition to perform basic research in a laboratory. Francis also liked the reputation Salk was creating for himself as an independent thinker.

Francis was willing to train the newcomer in his lab, where the two men could work to develop vaccines for viral diseases. Taking advantage of this opportunity, Jonas and his wife, Donna, packed their belongings and took a train to Ann Arbor.

The Japanese attack on America's naval forces in Pearl Harbor a few months before his arrival in Ann Arbor had altered everyone's lives. Salk wrote to Francis, suggesting that perhaps he should enlist in the war effort rather than doing research. Francis replied, however, that he would now focus on the development of an effective vaccine against the influenza virus, which had killed 850,000 Americans during an epidemic in 1918. As America began to gear up for World War II, the U.S. Army was particularly keen on finding a vaccine against influenza because American soldiers, more than any other group fighting in foreign countries, were thought to be susceptible to an influenza epidemic. Salk was eager to get started, and his enthusiasm was noted by Francis, who reported, "It was a busy time, the pressure was on, and Jonas fit right in." [21]

Salk began to make observations about how organisms develop resistance to the influenza infection. The best theory at the time held that the influenza virus caused chemical changes in the respiratory tissue

The Japanese attack Pearl Harbor in December 1941 began American involvement in World War II. Rather than enlist in the army, Salk supported the war effort by working on an influenza vaccine.

of those infected and that understanding this chemical change would be the key to finding a successful vaccine. Salk looked into the research that Francis had performed but was unable to determine if studying respiratory tissue or blood cells was the right path. Although Salk could not shed new light on this issue, in the process of studying the problem, he did make several unrelated discoveries.

In the process of experimenting with blood rather than respiratory tissue, Salk made a critical discovery relating to antibodies—molecules that animals produce in their blood to act as a defense against infectious diseases. Up until this time, doctors believed that any amount of antibodies, no matter how little, was sufficient to defend against a viral infection. To Salk's inquisitive mind, however, this theory did not make sense and he decided to investigate it.

What Salk discovered from his studies was that the degree of immunity to the influenza virus was related to the amount of influenza antibodies carried by the blood. The higher the concentration of antibodies, the greater the immunity. Salk was later to say, "Once it was established that antibody level was a reliable indicator of immunity, the problem was well in hand."[22] This important discovery quickly led to the discovery of yet another.

The next step for Salk was to discover a laboratory process to calculate the concentrations of antibodies in blood. Because antibodies are extremely small, determining their concentration in a blood sample cannot be accomplished by simply counting them. A virologist named George Hirst had discovered that influenza viruses caused red blood cells to clump together in test tubes. Scientists needing to know the concentration of antibodies in blood could now measure them by using a test based on the degree of blood clumping in a test tube. Although this discovery represented a significant advancement for influenza research, estimates often varied greatly.

Salk's passion for perfection motivated him to take a closer look at the clumping issue for the purpose of enabling scientists to make more reliable estimations. He discovered that the concentration could be more accurately calculated by using a mixture of chemicals that caused the clumping to become tighter and thus more accurately measured.

Salk next sought to understand why Francis's experimental killed influenza vaccines protected some of those who received the inoculations but not others. As Salk considered possible explanations for this imperfection, it occurred to him that since there were several different strains of the influenza virus, an effective vaccine should also contain several different strains of the influenza virus. As Francis and Salk moved forward with their research, Salk suggested that more strains of influenza virus be added to the vaccines to increase their effectiveness. This decision later created a highly effective vaccine. As Salk later bluntly stated, "To avoid . . . the failures so often ascribed to flu vaccines, you must cram your vaccine with every strain you can lay hands on."[23]

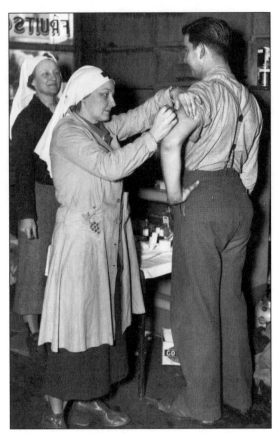

A man receives an early influenza vaccine. In Ann Arbor, Salk made several discoveries about how to improve influenza vaccines.

These three discoveries greatly enhanced Salk's reputation among the other virologists and immunologists with whom he worked in Ann Arbor. Francis also recognized Salk's success and elevated him to assistant director of the influenza research team. Whenever Francis was absent from the laboratory, Salk took charge. Salk later recalled this recognition with enthusiasm: "This was an active period in my life, at the age of twenty-nine I took over in Tom's [Francis] absence . . . it was quite a responsibility."[24]

THE NATURE OF A VIRUS

Viruses have always been more difficult for scientists to understand than most other microorganisms because they lack the internal structure found in all other living cells. In a sense half alive and half dead, viruses cannot reproduce, or replicate, without a living host that provides them with the chemicals that they need to replicate. Of all known organisms on earth, viruses are the smallest, varying in size from the largest of about 450 nanometers (0.000014 inches) to the smallest polioviruses of about 30 nanometers (about 0.000001 inches).

It is believed that viruses can remain in their resting state for thousands of years, maybe even millions. Without a living host, viruses drift in a lifeless form until they make contact with a host. Once contact is made, the virus either enters the cell directly or fuses to the cell membrane and injects its DNA into the host cell.

Once the genetic material of the virus has been transferred to the host, the virus has accomplished the first stage of the replication cycle. The virus uses various enzymes and proteins from the host, replicates itself, and completes the cycle by exiting the host cell. Some viruses exit the cell without killing it while other types lyse the cell membrane, meaning they the split open the cell, thereby killing it releasing newly formed virus particles ready to infect other cells. Still other viruses pass directly from one cell into an adjacent cell. The virus replication cycle ranges from two hours to several days.

Once viruses establish themselves in a plant or animal, they damage or kill the cells that they infect, causing a disease to spread throughout the infected host organism. A few viruses induce cells to grow uncontrollably, causing cancer. Some viruses kill cells by inflicting severe damage while others cause the cell to kill itself in response to the virus infection. This type of "cell suicide" is thought to be a host defense mechanism to eliminate infected cells before the virus can complete its replication cycle and spread to other cells. Depending upon the virus and the health of the host, organisms may survive virus infection and the virus may persist at low levels for the life of its host.

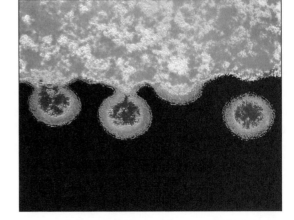

A virus infects a human host, as seen under a microscope

CONQUERING INFLUENZA

Salk was experiencing remarkable success as an assistant to Francis. In 1943, as their research on the influenza vaccine sped forward, the hotly debated question of whether the most effective vaccine should contain killed or live influenza viruses arose once again. Most leading virologists defended the use of live viruses in vaccines.

This view was based on a history of using live-virus vaccines. The live-virus technique had been successfully used in vaccines against the viral diseases smallpox, rabies, and yellow fever. Researchers recommending the use of the live-virus approach argued that weakened, or attenuated, viruses would produce a mild and harmless infection in the person inoculated. As these attenuated viruses spread throughout a person's body, the immune system would begin producing antibodies that would kill them. Then, if the virus that caused the disease were ever to return, the immune system would remember it and immediately produce the needed antibodies. The live-virus approach, however, included the risk that an inoculation of attenuated virus not properly weakened could trigger a robust infection that could overpower the person's immune system, causing the very disease it was intended to prevent. This had happened in the past.

Salk and Francis disagreed with the orthodox view, believing instead that the killed or inactivated viruses would produce a far more effective vaccine as well as a much safer one. They argued that living, infectious viruses were not needed to stimulate the human immune system to generate antibodies because killed, noninfectious viruses could trick the body into believing that they were alive. The killed or inactivated viruses retain their structure, which is what the immune system recognizes. This deception would stimulate the immune system to begin producing antibodies. Furthermore, and of significant consideration, employing the killed-virus technique would prevent any possibility of accidentally causing an epidemic of the disease they were trying to prevent.

The army agreed to allow Salk and Francis to test their influenza vaccine on several thousand troops. The tests were structured to determine if fewer soldiers who received the vaccine contracted influenza than an equal number of soldiers who did not receive the vaccine. In 1944 Salk completed the test and, after recording the results, concluded that 70 percent fewer soldiers who received the vaccine contracted influenza.

BREAKING AWAY

Francis had been a mentor and father figure to the younger Salk. However, toward the end of the war, as a successful vaccine moved into production, Salk began to feel constrained by their relationship. Salk and Francis worked well together and shared a mutual respect, yet each had differing ideas about how their research should proceed and about how the responsibility should be shared.

Following their successful killed-virus influenza vaccine for the army, Salk and Francis recorded their results in several publications. Salk's sense of success, as well as his sense of independence, led to a discussion between the two men over whose name should appear first on the publication. Francis, the senior man, placed his name first followed by Salk's name. Salk went to Francis asking that his name precede Francis's because Salk wanted the recognition and he felt he deserved it. Francis remembered Salk needling him with the comment, "Everybody knows who *you* are. It doesn't matter if your name is first or last."[25]

As time passed Salk began to feel that Francis was holding him back. Francis, from his point of view, believed Salk's intuitive leaps and apparent rush for results were introducing recklessness to his research. An argument between the two men broke out one day over a paper Salk asked Francis to read before it was submitted to a leading medical journal. Francis told Salk that the conclusions he had reached were not properly supported by good research evidence. This criticism caused Salk to walk away with the parting comment that he would publish it anyway. Francis, still the senior man, warned Salk that "if he did he had better go with it."[26] Francis meant that if Salk

published the paper, he would have to face the criticism of other scientists on his own.

Salk some years later recognized his impetuous and driving nature when talking with his biographer Richard Carter: "My striving was strong and unconcealed. I wanted to do independent work and I wanted to do it my *own way*. There may have been times when I made more of my data than might have been expected, but I was not functioning in the expected way."[27]

When the war ended in 1945, the army sent Salk to Germany to prepare for the possibility of an influenza epidemic as had following World War I in 1918. When none occurred, he returned to Ann Arbor. Upon his return from Europe Salk felt that the time had come for him to be in charge of his own research. He had mastered most of what was known about virology and immunology from Francis, but the young and talented researcher was ready for his own laboratory and eager to make his mark in life. In 1947 the University of Pittsburgh Medical School presented Salk with that opportunity.

3 The Opportunity Others Did Not See

Success at the University of Pittsburgh Medical School was viewed as highly improbable to everyone who knew about the offer except for Salk. The university, the laboratory facilities, even the city of Pittsburgh was each viewed by Salk's friends as a major step backward compared to what he would be leaving behind in Michigan. Salk, however, as was always the case, had a very different view. "I went down for a visit and saw nothing but opportunity. . . . What I was in love with, of course, was the prospect of independence."[28]

At thirty-three years old, it was time for Salk to make his mark in science. He had already learned more and achieved more than any of his colleagues, and as he departed Ann Arbor, he took with him optimism, enthusiasm, and, most of all, confidence. To Salk, adversity was simply the other side of opportunity. He vowed that he would do whatever it would take to do something significant to help humanity. At this stage in his life, Salk knew that he either would need to find a conventional path to success or make one of his own.

A RISKY MOVE

Everyone who knew Salk and of his offer to move to Pittsburgh warned him against ac-

cepting the position. Pittsburgh in those days was a filthy steel mill town covered in layers of dust and soot. Commuters were known to drive with their headlights on in the middle of the day because of the sooty skies. The families that owned the mills accumulated mountains of wealth, inspiring the quintessential American term "filthy rich." As the filth settled on the city, it created an unattractive environment as well as an unhealthy one.

The reputation of the University of Pittsburgh Medical School was not much better than the city's reputation. It was considered a place of academic mediocrity lacking modern laboratories and sufficient space for first-rate research. The dean of the medical school, Dr. William S. McEllroy, was attempting to shore up the school's status by attracting well-respected promising faculty members.

McEllroy invited Salk to visit the school. He was eager to have Salk join the faculty and offered him many incentives that included allowing him to develop his own research program and, what Salk sought most of all, independence. Salk viewed his arrival at Pittsburgh this way:

> I . . . went on to Pittsburgh, seeking again an opportunity to be somewhat

independent of my mentor [Dr. Francis]. The opportunity in Pittsburgh was something that others did not see, and I was advised against doing something as foolish as that because there was so little there. However, I did sense and see that there was an opportunity to do two things. One was to continue the work I was doing on influenza, and two, to begin to work on polio. [29]

As soon as Salk and his wife arrived in Pittsburgh, he saw firsthand that the research facilities compared poorly to those at Ann Arbor. The only research laboratory available was in the basement of a nearby public hospital, and it was only one-quarter the size he needed. To make matters worse, the laboratory was being used as a storage facility for all sorts of junk.

Although the sooty steel town of Pittsburgh, Pennsylvania (pictured), seemed an unlikely place for Salk to continue his medical research, he saw opportunity there.

Undaunted by the scope of the problem and unable to work without proper equipment, he scavenged instruments from other laboratories. Salk understood that a second-rate lab would not produce the results he would be looking for. After three months he finally managed to set up a basic laboratory where he could continue making discoveries as he had in Ann Arbor.

Of even greater disappointment than the laboratory situation was his hope for research independence. The independence he so desperately sought was denied him by a senior-level administrator, Dr. Lauffer, who refused to purchase some of the equipment that Salk requested. Dr. Lauffer was a plant virologist with no interest in Salk's research in human virology. Salk recognized the predicament he was in, and later described his feelings: "I was bound and gagged."[30]

To remedy the situation, Salk approached Dr. McEllroy, explained the problem, and requested that his title at the university be changed to one of higher status. Such a promotion would enable Salk to order all of his own equipment and to hire the technical staff he needed with the approval of McEllroy, rather than with the approval of Lauffer. McEllroy approved Salk's request. By asserting himself, Salk had once again seized control of the situation and moved ahead with his plans under circumstances that would have stifled the work of most scientists.

PERSISTENCE PAYS OFF

Salk's persistence in demanding better laboratory conditions had paid off. Now that he had made important headway acquiring the necessary laboratory equipment and had gained suitable research independence, Salk stood ready to complete an experiment he had started in Ann Arbor. Virologists are always searching for a technique to increase the potency of vaccines. Salk, along with others, discovered that various types of mineral oil solutions, properly prepared, could strengthen a vaccine. The significance of perfecting the mineral oil emulsion was that future vaccines could contain many more strains of viruses in a single inoculation. The trick to a successful solution was determining which oils were needed, the precise amounts of each oil, and how to properly assemble them. Applying his background in chemistry, Salk discovered the optimal mix of variables as well as the best process for producing the emulsion. Salk thrived on this sort of experimentation that required precise methodical thinking.

Fortunately for Salk, Dr. Harry M. Weaver at the National Foundation for Infantile Paralysis had heard of Salk's successful virus research. Weaver was the foundation's scientific director. He was responsible for determining how its research money would be spent. He believed that Salk was qualified to work on the poliovirus with foundation support.

POLIO RESEARCH AT LAST

Knowing the difficult circumstances Salk was working under, Weaver drove to Pittsburgh and asked Salk if he would be interested in a polio research project supported by foundation money. Weaver wanted

THE SHADOW DISEASE

At the start of the twentieth century, few people in America had ever heard of polio, but during the summer of 1916, the name of the disease was on everyone's lips. That was the year when a devastating epidemic struck the New York City area. By the end of the summer, twenty-seven thousand people were paralyzed and nine thousand were dead, yet no one knew what caused it. Panic gripped the population, and thousands of New Yorkers fled the city in order to avoid polio, although they had no idea what caused the disease.

Polio spread across America like a great shadow during the next several decades. By the 1940s dealing with the effects of polio became part of everyday life. No one was safe. Everybody knew someone infected by the most feared virus of the time, whether it was a family member, neighbor, or friend. Homes of polio victims were often labeled with large posters displaying in large red letters the warning, INFANTILE PARALYSIS—KEEP OFF THE STREET.

Ignorance about the disease caused people to panic. Irrational behavior became commonplace across America as parents sought to protect their children from the disease. During the height of one epidemic, some city councils ordered movie theaters, churches, schools, and other public places closed for one week. Social gatherings for children younger than fifteen also were banned. Because President Roosevelt had contracted polio the day he had gone swimming, many parents believed that the poliovirus spread in water. Soon many parents kept their children out of swimming pools. Drinking from a public water fountain was thought to be the cause at one time. Mothers cautioned their children and kept them at home with the commonly repeated words "Do as I tell you or you will end up in an iron lung."

The panic also caused irrational anti-social behavior. People began to distrust one another. Many stopped shaking hands for fear of catching polio. People became fearful of strangers and kept their children home from school if new children arrived. Some cities even bought a fogging device to spray the insecticide DDT in alleys.

A sign warns people that a child with polio lives inside this home.

three separate research teams to divide the work, and he wanted Salk to lead one team in Pittsburgh. To Salk, the offer represented the liberating opportunity he had been looking for since his arrival in Pittsburgh. Weaver even took the offer one step further by offering Salk the head research position on the project. Salk jumped at the offer even though he later admitted, "I had no experience in working with polio, but this provided me with an opportunity, just as the work on influenza did."[31]

How the Polio Virus Operates

Salk and other virologists knew that understanding how the poliovirus enters a person's body, and then their nerve cells, would give them valuable insight into the production of an effective vaccine. Many decades of research passed until virologists discovered that the poliovirus enters the human body through the nose and mouth. The virus moves through the stomach and enters the intestines. The lining of the intestines, which is highly specialized to extract and absorb nutrients from food, also proves to be a fertile area where the poliovirus first begins its invasion of the body's cells and subsequent reproduction or replication cycle.

As the poliovirus begins to replicate, some of the new viruses pass along the intestinal tract and are excreted. These shed viruses may then continue to infect other people if proper health standards are lacking. Some of those polioviruses that are not passed from the body travel through the blood to the spinal cord, part of the central nervous system. Once in the spinal cord, they continue to replicate.

It is in the nerve cells of the spinal cord that the poliovirus does its damage. The incubation period, the time from ingestion to the time of paralysis, is ten to fourteen days—slow compared to other viral diseases. James Hogle and his colleagues at Harvard University suspect that after attaching to the nerve cells, the poliovirus undergoes a series of changes that actually produce two intermediate forms. From the moment it attaches to its host's nervous system tissue, the poliovirus appears to make tiny adjustments in its protein shell that allow it to grab onto its host receptor cells more tightly. Once embedded, the virus creates temporary openings in its shell through which it throws out tiny protein threads, which embed in the host cell membrane. These threads not only anchor the virus to the cell, but also create pores for the poliovirus genetic material to enter.

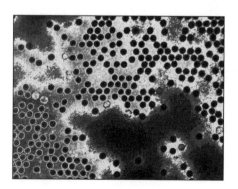

The poliovirus attacks a human cell, as seen under a microscope.

At the University of Pittsburgh, Salk (left) began working seriously on a polio vaccine.

At that time, scientists knew that polio was caused by more than one type of poliovirus. A successful polio vaccine would need to include all possible types. No one knew how many types might exist. There might be a hundred types or a handful; Weaver proposed to find out. Weaver knew that typing a large number of poliovirus strains would take many years. The task required perseverance and perfection to ensure the accurate typing of all strains. According to Richard Carter, everyone involved in the typing of the poliovirus agreed with Weaver that "no single problem in all of the medical sciences was more uninteresting to solve. The solution necessi-

tated the monotonous repetition of exactly the same technical procedures on virus after virus seven days a week, fifty-two weeks a year, for three solid years." [32] Salk was confident about his ability to do this work; he accepted the challenge: "Weaver represented a liberating force. Weaver came along, willing to provide me with funds and work and people and facilities to be administered and organized by me. This was liberation." [33]

Three researchers, Drs. Isabel Morgan, Howard Howe, and David Bodian of Johns Hopkins Medical School in Baltimore, Maryland, had already established the existence of at least three distinct antigenic types of poliovirus, meaning three types of the virus capable of stimulating the body to produce antibodies. However, these researchers suspected there might be more. No one could know for certain until more than one hundred unidentified strains of poliovirus could be assigned to one of those three, or possibly more, antigenic types.

True to his character, Salk saw the task of typing each poliovirus strain as an excellent opportunity, not as a monotonous task. Donna Salk, who had by this time shared many disappointments as well as triumphs with her husband, made this observation about the qualities that made him ideal for such a task: "He wants nothing second rate. . . . This perfection seems to consume and exhaust him. . . . He can't work any other way."[34] As Salk himself said:

> That experience was looked upon by most people as just a routine drudgery. It wasn't that way to me, because instantly I saw that there were more efficient ways of typing viruses than were proposed by those who set forth the protocol that I was supposed to follow. It didn't take long for them to realize, as well as myself, that I saw the world differently, and that I could make things work more efficiently, and effectively.[35]

Salk understood what many researchers failed to see; typing the poliovirus was merely a first step toward development of a polio vaccine. He realized that whoever first completed the tedious work of typing the virus would have the inside track on the development of a vaccine—the ultimate goal.

ASSERTING AN UNORTHODOX VIEW

Shortly after Salk's thirty-fourth birthday, he began preliminary work on typing the poliovirus. This fundamental research brought national prestige to the medical school. Salk was promoted to the senior position of research professor of bacteriology. He had developed a reputation as a quick learner and problem solver, but even his extensive background could not prepare him for what lay ahead.

The poliovirus only grows naturally in two animals, humans and monkeys. As a result, all experiments had to be conducted on monkeys. This required large cages, cleaning crews, veterinarians, barrels of expensive fruit, and a large budget to pay for them. Salk estimated the need for 30,000 monkeys of the rhesus and java species found in India and the Philippines. Although only 17,500 were actually used, the university had to hire trappers to catch the animals and had to procure a special license to export such a large monkey population. At $30 per monkey, Salk's budget for the poliovirus typing project was quickly running low.

In 1948 a formal meeting that would set the tone for the research team kicked off the poliovirus typing project. The dominant view of proper procedure was first to inject monkeys with one of the three known virus types, I, II, or III, and then to infect each monkey with an unknown virus to determine if the unknown type matched the type first injected. For example, a monkey that had recovered from an injection of type III virus would then be injected with an unknown strain to determine if the unknown virus was also a type III. If the monkey recovered, the unknown strain was a type III, but if it contracted polio, then the unknown strain was a type I or II. Then the experiment would be repeated until researchers could determine which of the three types the unknown strain belonged to. To further complicate this procedure, the dose level was a critical variable and no one knew how to control it.

While politely listening to the discussion among the three teams, Salk returned to one of his most important views concerning science: the application of clear logic, rather than orthodox beliefs, could often uncover a more efficient approach. After the meeting ended, Salk thanked everyone for their ideas and isolated himself in his office to rethink the typing problem.

Salk determined that the most efficient process would be to do just the opposite of what the committee had recommended. Salk wanted to start by injecting uninfected monkeys with a large dose of an unknown poliovirus strain. When an infection took hold, an antibody would be produced in the

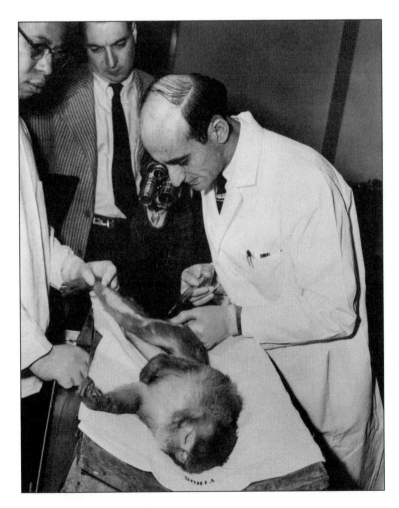

A scientist injects a monkey with the polio vaccine. Salk proposed a new method for using monkeys in polio research.

Dr. Albert Sabin criticized Salk's research approach.

reach final agreement on the process to be used for typing the poliovirus. Salk shocked the audience by proposing his idea, which was in opposition to the majority attending the meeting.

Dr. Albert Sabin, a senior virologist who had been working with poliovirus for many years, was especially critical of Salk's approach. During a meeting of the full committee, Salk asked a question that infuriated Sabin, who commented, "Dr. Salk! You should know better than to ask that question." Sabin was implying that the question was too foolish to be given serious consideration. The insult stung Salk to the point that he later described Sabin's remark as "like being kicked in the teeth. I could *feel* the resistance and the hostility and the disapproval. I never attended another one of those meetings afterwards without the same feeling."[36] This jab was the first in a lifetime of conflict between the two men.

TYPING THE POLIOVIRUS

Following the New York meeting, Salk returned to Pittsburgh to begin the task of typing the poliovirus using his procedure, even though his view was still opposed by the majority of those attending the meeting. Regarding his difference of opinion with the other scientists, Salk later said, "What could I do? I couldn't slap those people in the face and call them dumb bunnies and shriek that they were doing their job ass-wise [backward]. . . . I went ahead and did what I pleased and ignored the committee."[37]

By the fall of 1949, roughly one year following the New York meeting, Salk told a

animal's blood to inactivate the virus. Researchers could then check the monkeys' blood to determine which of the antibodies had been produced. From this information, they would know which of the three known viruses had been inactivated and thereby which type the unknown virus belonged to.

The wonderful opportunity that Salk saw when he accepted his Pittsburgh position in 1947 was soon to be put to the test. Six months following the kick-off meeting, the same group of scientists met in New York to reporter that he would soon finish the poliovirus typing, two years ahead of time. Although Salk had stepped on the toes of Sabin and several other senior scientists, he eventually demonstrated the merits of his procedure.

Salk and the other two teams had successfully proved, using the most rigorous scientific standards possible, that all one hundred of the poliovirus strains tested did indeed belong to one of the three known polioviruses types. Type I comprised 82 percent of the strains; type II, 10 percent; and type III, 8 percent. Dr. John Rodman Paul, professor of preventative medicine at Yale University and a member of the Polio Hall of Fame, called Salk's successful poliovirus typing research "the single greatest piece of development research that the National Foundation for Infantile Paralysis

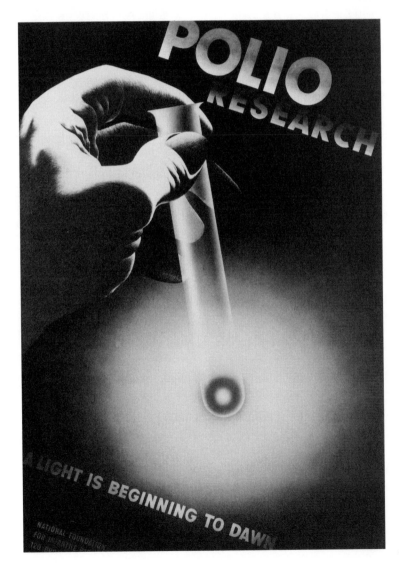

The National Foundation for Infantile Paralysis used posters like this one to advertise the need for polio research.

Curing Polio One Dime at a Time

Polio research was an expensive proposition. Without massive funding, little progress could be made. When President Franklin Delano Roosevelt established the National Foundation for Infantile Paralysis (NFIP), its primary objectives were to help support polio victims around the nation and support research into the poliovirus to find a safe and effective vaccine.

The director of the NFIP called on some of Hollywood's biggest stars to help organize fundraising campaigns across America. Almost immediately, the comedian Eddie Cantor proposed using his radio show to solicit donations from average Americans. A popular newsreel feature of the period was called "The March of Time," and Cantor proposed calling the fundraising campaign the "The March of Dimes," with the idea of asking each listener to mail a dime to the White House to help fight polio.

The first appeal for the March of Dimes was aired during the last week of January 1938. Eddie Cantor and Clayton Moore, a radio actor from the *Lone Ranger,* appealed to the nation's children to contribute dimes to help fight the disease that had crippled and killed so many other children.

Two days after the broadcast, a flood of letters arrived at the White House, each containing a dime. The first day following the broadcast, 30,000 letters were received. The next day, 50,000 letters showed up. Then 150,000 letters arrived. Since the radio program was a favorite of children, many of the letters arrived with peanut butter and jelly smudges. When all of the letters were opened, O'Connor discovered that his new foundation had raised $1.8 million, $268,000 of which had been mailed to the White House one dime at a time.

Following this record-breaking fundraiser, the March of Dimes became an independent organization dedicated to raising money for polio research. Major Hollywood stars of the time toured the country to collect more dimes, and soon March of Dimes money collectors became a common sight in airports, bus stations, and supermarkets. Much of the money that funded polio research and vaccine production came from the millions of dimes the organization collected.

was to accomplish during the years of its existence."[38]

Although Salk would take two more years to retest all the results in order to confirm the findings, he was now ready to move to the next level of polio research, which was to find a vaccine capable of treating all three poliovirus types.

Taking Charge

Two years after arriving at the University of Pittsburgh Medical School, Salk appeared to be at the pinnacle of his career. He had overcome all of the obstacles that his colleagues had warned him would be insurmountable. The creative methods that he applied first to complete the mineral oil emulsion and then the typing of the poliovirus had given him a reputation for success.

As Salk's list of accomplishments grew, however, opposition to him also grew. Dealing with the criticism became another challenge that Salk would need to face.

Half of the problem rested with those colleagues who disagreed with his ideas. Some of them felt threatened by his unorthodox approach to problem solving; some were envious of his success and recognition; some were offended because he was now pushing ahead with little regard for the opinions of those who disagreed with his scientific approach; and some disliked his confident and sometimes aloof personality.

The other half of the problem rested with Salk. At this stage in his life, he had overcome many obstacles that he knew would have stymied lesser scientists, and he was becoming less reticent about stating his opinions. Author Jane Smith comments that: "Salk sometimes had difficulty dealing with people of divergent scientific thinking, but he got along very well with those who agreed to make his interests and scientific opinions their own."[39] Salk had to learn how to accommodate criticism. Realizing that he could not simply dismiss the differing views and ideas of his colleagues, Salk took the advice of Dr. Thomas Francis to listen to the ideas of his adversaries and to learn how to involve them in the pursuit of their shared goal: the development of a successful vaccine against polio.

4 Building with the Help of Others

With the typing program well on the way to completion, Salk began to think about how to develop a killed poliovirus vaccine. Time was of the essence. When Salk went to his laboratory in the basement of the Pittsburgh hospital, he sometimes walked through the polio ward to visit patients—mostly young children—who were suffering terribly and even dying. Salk was moved by their plight and felt compelled to find an answer as quickly as possible.

The time of the lone medical researcher working in isolation was long over. The complexity and scope of the problems now being worked on were too great for an individual to do alone. Scientists had to keep abreast of the work being done in other laboratories. Important advances would often be made by building on the work of others. Journal articles, scientific conferences, and formal and informal collaboration all played roles in this communication among scientists. The cost of personnel, equipment, and supplies was too large to be borne without substantial outside support. Scientists had to apply for grants from both public and private sources.

FINDING MONEY

One man in particular, Basil O'Connor, was in a position to direct large sums of money for polio research, and for this reason everyone involved in polio research cultivated his friendship. O'Connor was a longtime friend and law partner of Franklin Delano Roosevelt before Roosevelt became president of the United States. When Roosevelt approached O'Connor about setting up a charitable fund to help fight polio, O'Connor committed all of his energies to raising money as chairman of the National Foundation for Infantile Paralysis (NFIP).

Salk struck up a friendship with O'Connor while the two men were returning home on the ocean liner *Queen Mary* from the International Conference on Poliomyelitis in Denmark. Both men had a great deal in common. Each had known the poverty of the immigrant experience, yet each had risen to a position of respect by virtue of hard work and focused attention. Of greater importance, however, each had little patience for conventional thinkers.

O'Connor was eager to provide financial assistance and was supportive of Salk's requests for grants from the NFIP. Salk quickly increased his staff from a few assistants to a group of fifty, including scientists with experience in virology and immunology. The NFIP gave Salk funding to expand and upgrade his laboratory. Hoping to find not only a way to prevent polio but also a cure for his daughter, Betty Ann, who had recently contracted the disease, O'Conner made it clear to Salk as well as other recipients of NFIP funds that he was looking for "a planned Miracle."[40]

The amount of money Salk received from the NFIP rankled some other polio researchers who felt they also had a right to such a large sum. Allegations by rival polio research teams suggested that O'Conner had shown inappropriate favoritism. Salk recognized that without O'Connor's faith in his pursuits, "the polio vaccine would have been obstructed for years."[41]

CULTURING THE POLIO VIRUSES

With funding in place, Salk returned to his research. He had several problems to solve in order to develop a killed-virus vaccine.

Salk (left) and Basil O'Connor participate in a 1950s radio broadcast. O'Connor provided Salk with much-needed money to continue researching the polio vaccine.

The first problem was how to grow very large quantities of the three poliovirus types other than in the live nerve tissue of monkeys and humans. For obvious reasons, humans could not be sacrificed to grow the viruses, and as Salk reflected on the 17,500 monkeys that had been used in his poliovirus typing tests, he realized that using thousands more for growing the viruses was an unthinkable undertaking. In fact, there were not enough monkeys in existence to grow the amount of poliovirus that eventually would be needed to inoculate the entire population of the United States. Besides, monkeys were expensive, difficult to keep alive in a laboratory setting, in low supply, and they had to be killed once they contracted polio.

THE NOT-SO-GLAMOROUS LIFE OF A POLIO POSTER CHILD

Each year during the polio epidemic, the March of Dimes selected a young polio victim, both legs in braces, to be photographed heroically smiling while standing with crutches. The photo was published in thousands of magazines and newspapers to evoke public sympathy for the annual March of Dimes fundraising season. When Diane Kirlin was six years old, she was chosen to be the poster child for 1956. Forty-three years later, on February 23, 1999, Kirlin told her story to reporter Huntly Collins of the *Philadelphia Inquirer* newspaper: "From her hospital bed, Diane Kirlin couldn't see the rows of iron lungs. But she could hear them—a great *swishing* sound just beyond her cubicle at Philadelphia's Hospital for Contagious Diseases. 'When the nurses would, turn one off, you knew that a child had died. Then they would roll the iron lung away,' she recalled. At age 6, Diane became a March of Dimes poster child. With her long ringlets, frilly dresses, and custom-made white shoes, she was a picture-perfect little girl—in braces and crutches. She was photographed with Phillies pitcher Curt Simmons. She went on the *Chief Halftown* television show. She pleaded for more donations to support research and medical care for children like herself."

But behind the smiling face, Diane seethed. "My mother loved it," Diane recalled. "She loved showing me off. I didn't. I wanted to be just like everybody else." In 1956, Diane was sent to a hospital for crippled children for corrective surgery on her hips and knees. She did not leave for seven months. No visitors were allowed, not even her parents. On Sundays, at the appointed time, she went to the window of her fourth-floor room and looked down. There, waving up to her, were her mother and father.

After she was discharged, Diane ended up at the city's school for crippled children because the city's public and parochial schools would not enroll her. "All I wanted to do," she said, "was to wear a uniform and go to school with my brother and sister." The closest she got to that was her first communion when a neighborhood boy drove her up to the church in a station wagon. "I felt so proud because I was like everybody else."

Physician John Enders and two others were the first to discover how to culture live poliovirus outside the human body.

In mid-July 1950, Salk learned of the pioneering work of doctors John Enders, Thomas Weller, and Fred Robbins, who had discovered how to grow poliovirus in vitro, meaning in glass dishes. Culturing live viruses outside the body of a living animal was a revolutionary scientific breakthrough, and Enders, Weller, and Robbins later received the Nobel Prize for their discovery.

Salk thought that the in vitro technique might be the key to developing the large quantities of poliovirus needed for a killed polio vaccine. He put his team to work to see if they could duplicate Enders' experiment. Salk hoped that he would soon be producing cultures of poliovirus for use in vaccines.

The Salk team attempted to duplicate Enders' work with human embryonic tissue, but failed. After much trial and error, the Salk team finally succeeded using tissue from the testicles of monkeys. The amount of virus that could be cultivated in vitro using the testicles of a single monkey was equivalent to the amount of virus they could grow in two hundred living monkeys. Salk gave credit to the Enders' team while speaking at an international polio convention in Copenhagen: "The work that he [Enders] has done stands out in the last years as one of the most outstanding contributions in poliovirus poliomyelitis research. It has been possible, simply by following Dr. Enders' technique . . . to isolate viruses quite readily."[42] The ability to culture viruses in vitro solved the first technical problem and freed Salk to move on to the next.

KILLED-VIRUSES REVISITED

The debate over a polio vaccine made of live or killed viruses continued. Sabin was committed to the use of the live-virus technique, as were other virologists. Salk, however, leaned toward using killed viruses. Salk had encountered this question while in medical school and had explored it further in his work with Thomas Francis.

Although Salk felt confident that the killed virus was the better solution for polio, his position was largely theoretical. He knew a killed virus had worked with the influenza vaccine and logic dictated that it would work with polio, but he had not yet proved that theory. Other scientists had tried to develop killed-virus polio vaccines but without evidence of success until the work of another leading virologist, Dr. Isabel Morgan.

Morgan was a veteran poliovirus researcher. She was a member of the team at Johns Hopkins Medical School that had contributed to the identification of the three types of polioviruses that Salk later confirmed during the typing project. Morgan had succeeded where others had failed in using the killed-virus technique in inoculating monkeys. After inoculation the concentration of antibodies found in the blood of the monkeys was the same as was produced with live viruses. Morgan had cultured the poliovirus using monkey spinal cord tissue and then killed the poliovirus

with a formaldehyde solution known as formalin. Formaldehyde had been used for years in biological and medical laboratories as a disinfectant and as a preserving solution for animal tissue.

Although Morgan succeeded with the killed virus in monkeys, duplicating that success in humans might not be so simple. Although the physiology of monkeys and humans is very similar, transferring medical procedures that work successfully on one species to the other is often burdened with problems. First, the likelihood of a severe reaction to the vaccine was high. Additionally, polio is not a naturally occurring disease in monkeys, which caused skeptics to doubt that humans would experience the same immune response. Many respected doctors and virologists argued that if a killed-virus vaccine caused antibody development in a monkey, it was because the virus had not really been killed.

As far as Salk was concerned, the results Morgan achieved were similar to those he had anticipated. Salk recognized that Morgan's work had the potential for being revolutionary, but it would need to be refined and improved before a practical vaccine could be made. While Sabin and others who championed the live-virus approach issued dire warnings against using the killed virus, Salk believed he could perfect a killed-virus vaccine for humans.

PERFECTING THE KILLED-VIRUS PROCESS

Salk was by no means a newcomer to the formalin treatment of viruses. He had first

Dr. Albert Sabin

Dr. Albert Sabin was born in Poland in 1906 and immigrated to New York City in 1921 with his parents. In 1931 he received his M.D. degree from New York University. After working at the Rockefeller Institute, he joined the staff of the Children's Hospital Research Foundation and the College of Medicine of the University of Cincinnati.

Sabin's most noted discovery was his live-virus polio vaccine at the end of the 1950s. It was initially tested in Russia and after it was demonstrated to be effective, it was approved for use in the United States in late 1961. By the mid 1960s Sabin's vaccine, orally administered in sugar cubes, had replaced Salk's injected vaccine as the most commonly used polio vaccine in the world. Sabin's vaccine was primarily used in third world nations.

Today, many countries are using both Sabin's and Salk's vaccines. The World Health Organization hopes to eradicate polio worldwide by 2010 using a combination of the two vaccines. In February 1999 virologists J.M. Oliver and B. Aylward, in the *Bulletin of the World Health Organization*, praised Dr. Sabin: "This would be a fitting tribute to Sabin, who was not only a great scientist, but also a great benefactor. He did not patent the 'Sabin strains,' but made them freely available to all vaccine producers capable of making effective use of them. In 1972, in an unprecedented gesture, Dr. Sabin donated these strains to the World Health Organization to increase their availability in developing countries."

Scientists who study immunology say that the oral polio vaccine was only one of Sabin's victories. He also found ways to combat the dengue fever, Japanese encephalitis, and he developed an aerosol vaccine against measles. In his later years, he worked to conquer AIDS.

Before Sabin's death in 1993, he had received forty-six honorary degrees from U.S. and foreign universities as well as the U.S. National Medal of Science, the Presidential Medal of Freedom, the Medal of Liberty, the Order of Friendship Among Peoples award from the Soviet Union, and many more from several South American countries.

Sabin administers his oral polio vaccine.

learned about the use of formalin in Ann Arbor where his mentor, Dr. Francis, had already developed a formalin formula for the killed-virus procedure. Morgan's work had furthered the science of the formalin inactivation of viruses by further refinement of the components. Salk believed he could improve on this procedure for producing the killed poliovirus.

The trick to perfecting the formalin formula as well as its application to viruses was to make sure the viruses were completely killed but not entirely obliterated. This was a dicey proposition because if even the most minute amount of live virus survived in the vaccine that would be used for inoculations, the person receiving the shot could develop a case of paralytic polio. If, on the other hand, the formalin process damaged the viruses' structure, they would fail to activate the human immune system that develops the needed antibodies.

Salk set to work to make an exact science of the formalin-inactivation process. He experimented with the proportions of each ingredient, the optimal temperature at which the formalin would be exposed to the viruses, the length of time for the exposure, and the optimal temperature for storage.

During the winter of 1951–52, Salk experimented with many variations before he found a workable combination of variables. Salk also concluded that the tissue from monkey kidneys was better for growing the poliovirus in vitro than was the tissue from their testes.

Because increasing the nutrient content of the medium might further increase the yield of viruses during the in vitro culturing process, Salk contracted with Dr. Ray-

Salk, at work in his laboratory, was certain he could produce a killed-virus polio vaccine for humans.

mond Parker of the Connaught Laboratory in Toronto to provide a nutrient called Medium-199. This nutrient allowed Salk to cultivate the poliovirus in large quantities. Salk used it to manufacture one quart of polio vaccine—more than anyone else had succeeded in manufacturing.

Salk believed that as a chemist he could understand the nature of the inactivation process and that as a virologist he could understand how the poliovirus would react to the vaccine. After relatively little testing Salk believed he knew intuitively how the vaccine would work. Whether he was arrogant or supremely confident in his intellect is difficult to judge. However, Dr. Walter Eckhart, a longtime colleague, said in an interview, "Jonas liked to use his imagination to gain insight. For example, when he thought about viruses, he might imagine himself as a virus to see what obstacles the virus had to overcome to survive and grow in its host."[43]

Bridging Monkeys and Humans

Nowadays, the leap between experimenting with monkeys and experimenting with humans is a long one. If experiments go wrong and a few monkeys die, there are usually few complaints. The same, however, cannot be said of humans, especially when children are the subjects of the experiments. Although fewer regulations were in place in the 1950s, it was still a difficult step to move from animal to human studies.

Salk was ready to test his vaccine on humans, but he understood that unless he had support from his colleagues, he would encounter a terrible outcry that might find its way to the nation's media. If that happened, he knew he could anticipate public objection to risking the health of children. On December 4, 1951, there would be a meeting in New York of all scientists working on polio

Dr. Thomas Rivers supported Salk's desire to test the polio vaccine on humans.

vaccines. Salk decided that this would be an opportunity to raise the issue. His only uncertainty was over the most diplomatic approach to use to suggest that human testing should begin.

Salk received some unexpected support even before he raised the issue. Dr. Thomas Rivers, a research scientist at the Rockefeller Institute and coworker with Basil O'Connor, stood up at the conference and said, "I think it is time that we got ready to go somewhere, and somebody ought to come up with some concrete experiments that will be done in human beings on a small scale in order to get going."[44] Salk was delighted with Rivers' comment because it presented him with an opening to introduce his ideas about human testing. As it turned out, he was the only member who had come prepared with a proposal for human testing. Salk received tentative support from one or two other members, but he also received a great deal of criticism from Sabin.

While the debate shifted back and forth, an unexpected incident occurred. Amid the expressions of concern for recklessly injecting children with polio vaccine, Dr. Howard Howe of Johns Hopkins Medical School rose to address the members of the meeting with these sobering words: "Since many people have said it is high time that we ought to try some human volunteers, it gives me courage to tell you that some have been tried and the results are very tentative. That is why I hesitate to say very much about them."[45]

This pronouncement created pandemonium in the meeting and triggered an immediate and tumultuous debate. Such an act was viewed by nearly everyone as being both reckless and unethical. Sabin, more than anyone else, stridently objected to the risks involved in such an experiment on humans, and many of his colleagues agreed. Part of the dispute arose over the fact that Howe had used the killed-virus technique that Sabin had always believed to be dangerous. Members shouted accusations back and forth across the conference room floor, and the debate became so heated that Howe finally told everyone that he would provide details of his experiment to all members. The meeting then abruptly ended.

Salk's ability to build on the results of others continued. He might now be able to accelerate his research based on what he could learn from Howe. Howe's inoculation of six patients made Howe the object of criticism rather than himself. Although Howe's results were inconclusive, he had given Salk the best present he could have asked for—someone else to absorb the criticism for bridging the testing gap between monkeys and human beings.

THE ADJUVANT

During the shouting that took place at the December 4 meeting, Sabin had been especially agitated about Howe's use of a mineral oil supplement called an adjuvant. The purpose of the adjuvant was to increase the potency of the vaccine.

Creating a vaccine with an adjuvant meant adding mineral oil to the water used as a suspension fluid for the virus. The advantage of adding mineral oil to the water

SUGAR CUBES

The popularity of Sabin's vaccine among the general population of the world stemmed from the fact that it was suspended in sugar cubes and administered orally—a relief from the three shots that the Salk vaccine required. Each sugar cube, saturated with a drop, or about one-fourth of a cubic centimeter, of live-virus vaccine, was simply eaten. Sabin's vaccine could be administered by anyone, unlike the Salk vaccine that had to be injected through a syringe by a trained medical practitioner.

Avoiding the pain of a shot, however, was not the issue. During the 1960s, poor countries throughout the world, lacking an efficient network of hospitals and trained medical staff, could turn over the responsibility of dispensing the sugar to teachers and parents. Injecting vaccines with syringes and needles required expensive medical staff and always ran risks of administering only partial injections of the vaccine as well as transferring infectious diseases from improperly sterilized needles or shared needles.

In addition to the simplicity and safety of dispensing the Sabin vaccine on sugar cubes, the cost was also significantly less than the needle and syringe required for the Salk vaccine—an important consideration especially when millions of children in poor countries need the vaccine. The price of administering the vaccine-saturated sugar cubes was a matter of pennies per dose.

To some scientists, a third advantage of the Sabin vaccine over the Salk vaccine was also compelling. People who took the oral live-virus vaccine harbored a protective virus that could, under some circumstances, be passed to others through the environment by coming in contact with that person's feces. As distasteful as this may seem to those living in modern sanitized surroundings, it is nonetheless a second-hand transfer of the vaccine from somebody who had eaten the sugar cube.

Sabin's live-virus vaccine is not, however, without drawbacks. The live-virus in the vaccine does cause polio in a small number of inoculated children—about one in every three hundred thousand. Also, some children who already have problems with weak immune systems cannot risk ingesting the live-virus form of the vaccine because it may actually overwhelm their immune systems and cause paralysis. Additionally, in warm, humid environments such as the tropics, the live-virus vaccine appears to be less effective because of interference with other intestinal viruses.

In 1960 after preliminary trials, Sabin's sugar cubes were first used on about 100 million people in Russia. It was approved for use in the United States, and in late 1961 Americans of all ages received them. It is estimated that the worldwide use of Sabin's sugar cubes soaked with his live-virus vaccine has prevented about 5 million cases of paralytic polio and about a half-million deaths.

was that when injected the mineral oil forms a bubble under the skin. This bubble of oil slowly releases the virus into the bloodstream and extends the production of antibodies over a longer period of time than does water without oil.

Adjuvants were not new to Salk; he had used them in experimental influenza vaccines. When inoculating humans with any substance foreign to the human body, anything can happen. Howe had experimented with different types of oils and found that the viscosity—the thickness of the oil—was a factor in improving the release of the viruses into the body. In addition to the timed release, Howe had to ensure that the composition of the oil would not adversely affect the virus.

Like all scientists, Salk benefited a great deal from the experiments of others. Part of Salk's genius was his ability to recognize potentially valuable medical discoveries and build on them. As 1952 moved forward briskly, Salk was eager to test his vaccine.

Chapter

5 A Shot in the Arm

Salk and his team had been laboring for five exhausting years amid the howls of monkeys and scientists alike. Everyone was burned out from the tedium associated with benchwork—the day-to-day labor at benches covered with glass vials of chemicals, glass tubing, Bunsen burners, and racks of test tubes used for culturing viruses. Salk, as much as anyone, needed an invigorating boost of morale in order to continue the push toward a vaccine. One technician in the group likened the rigorous work pace to the day and night forced marches that General George Patton imposed on American soldiers as they pushed across Europe toward Germany during World War II.

Salk and his staff were also in need of a literal shot in the arm—a human arm. Salk was constantly aware of the numbers of children who died from polio each day. Anxious to set in motion life-saving inoculations for millions of children throughout the world, he looked for an opportunity to inject his vaccine into the first human volunteers.

THE D.T. WATSON HOME

For safety reasons, Salk wanted the first human subjects to be polio victims who would not be at risk for getting the disease again. Although he was confident, from studies in monkeys, that the experimental vaccine preparations did not contain living viruses, he was a physician and was cautious about moving into human subjects. He planned to test vaccines containing only either type I, type II, or type III killed poliovirus in subjects who already had antibodies against the same poliovirus type (homotypic antibody).

Although it was common practice at the time, Salk was reluctant to use prisoners or mental patients as the first human subjects. He thought that polio patients and their families would be most motivated to volunteer and to provide blood samples for several months after vaccination. Through a colleague at the University of Pittsburgh, Salk was introduced to Dr. Jessie Wright, a leading authority on polio rehabilitation. In addition to other activities, she was the medical director of the D.T. Watson Home for Crippled Children in Leetsdale, a suburb of Pittsburgh.

The Watson Home was a mansion that once belonged to the wealthy Watson family. They had donated their estate to be used as a temporary residence for disadvantaged children. For many years it had

In 1952 Salk expanded his polio research from the laboratory to the D.T. Watson Home where he conducted the first human trials.

been a place where children could live while learning to adjust to various physical handicaps. After the beginning of large polio outbreaks, most of the residents were young polio patients.

Wright knew of Salk's studies in animals, and together they presented the proposal to the directors and staff of the Watson Home. Part of the proposal was that the human trials be kept secret. Salk knew that news of human studies would generate a lot of public speculation, and he wanted to make sure that the results were complete before he presented them to other scientists. He did not want to experience what Howard Howe

had experienced the previous December when Howe had been forced to share preliminary results that he was not yet sure were accurate.

In May 1952, Salk learned that the staff at the Watson Home agreed to support the studies and that the patients and their families were willing to participate. At this time, Salk's work schedule shifted into high gear. The idea of tests on children with polio spurred him forward to the point where a one-hour Sunday walk was the extent of his weekly diversion from the laboratory. One of his colleagues recalled the laboratory atmosphere this way:

"Hurry Up and Do Something"

Dr. Salk worked such long hours in his laboratory that many who did not know him incorrectly concluded that he was remote and unmoved by the suffering of the children who contracted the dreaded poliovirus. Two nurses working in the hospital where Salk worked made these comments to Richard Carter for his book, Breakthrough, *regarding Salk's understanding of those who suffered:*

"He certainly knew what was going on upstairs [in the polio wards], and anyone who understands how sensitive he is to suffering can imagine how all of his scientific and technical problems must have goaded him under those circumstances. He knew that children were dying within a few yards of him because the problems had not yet been solved. A lot of people thought he was an awfully cold fish. They thought he was remote from the everyday life of the hospital and indifferent to it. This was unfair. His job was to understand polio, not to treat it. He knew what polio did to people and their families. He had been present often enough when decisions were made to remove a child from a respirator because she was going to die anyhow and someone else might benefit from the apparatus."

Another nurse working in the same polio ward added, "And I can remember how the staff used to kid Dr. Salk—kidding in earnest—telling him to hurry up and do something."

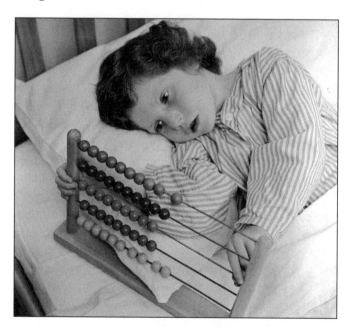

Despite some criticism, Salk was intimately aware of the plight of young polio victims.

We worked like dogs. It was like a factory but those of us who knew how unusual that kind of speed-up was in a university lab did not mind, because we felt we were part of a closely knit team engaged in a great effort. The bravery he [Salk] was showing in going ahead so rapidly towards human experiments was also terribly admirable, we felt.[46]

On June 12, 1952, Salk and his staff visited the Watson Home to draw the first blood samples. Many of the children's parents had agreed to let them participate in the testing of Salk's new vaccine. Everyone also promised not to discuss the experiment with the newspapers. Salk's plan was to watch for side effects of the inoculation and to determine whether his vaccine could increase the level of antibodies already in patients' systems. He wanted to find out if the killed virus would still be recognized by the human immune system. Success for Salk would be the observation of significant increases in the childrens' antibodies.

I'VE GOT IT

Salk drew blood samples from forty-five children and twenty-seven staff members. Back at his laboratory in Pittsburgh, each blood sample was tested for the specific type of poliovirus. Salk returned on July 2 with syringes filled with the pink-colored vaccine and inoculated a small group of patients with homotypicvaccine—vaccine containing poliovirus of the same type as the antibodies in each person. Although Salk was always a man of confidence, he understood the inherent dangers of experimentation on humans. Following the inoculations, Salk confessed, "When you inoculate children with a polio vaccine, you don't sleep well for two or three months."[47]

Salk returned to the Watson Home that same night to check on everyone and called every day following the inoculations. No unusual reactions were reported. He became a regular visitor to the home and impressed everyone there with his dedication and kindness toward the children. When Salk observed no negative reactions, he began to test vaccine preparations with more than one virus type and with or without adjuvant. He now included subjects who had not had paralytic polio: Watson Home patients with other conditions, Watson Home staff, and members of the patients' families. A second study was begun at the Polk State School for mentally challenged children and adults.

Toward the end of the summer, when Salk performed final testing on blood collected from each person after vaccination, he found that each had elevated levels of the antibodies against the virus type they originally had—just as he had predicted. Of even greater joy for Salk was finding that each subject also now had antibodies against virus types they did not previously have—just what he had hoped to see. That evening when Salk returned home, he turned to his wife, Donna, and three sons—Peter, age eight; Darrell, age five; and Jonathan, age two—and tersely remarked as he settled into a chair, "I've got it."[48]

Now he had evidence that the vaccine could produce antibodies in humans, and he had a good idea about the mixture of types and the amount of killed poliovirus

Salk, his wife, and three sons were among the first to receive the polio vaccine.

to use. Although he had not shown that the vaccine would keep people from getting polio, he knew that the vaccine was safe and that the antibodies in the blood had a chance of being effective. As soon as possible, he vaccinated himself, as well as all the members of his laboratory, who worked daily with dangerous live polioviruses. He also inoculated his wife and three sons.

Years later Salk reflected on his decision to innoculate himself, his family, and his staff well before widespread use of the vaccine could begin. In an interview in 1987 in the *Wall Street Journal*, Salk described what he had done, saying, "I looked upon it as ritual and symbolic. You wouldn't do unto others that which you wouldn't do unto yourself."[49]

Salk knew that now he would need to announce his success with the Watson Home subjects to his colleagues. He knew his adversaries, especially Sabin, would fly into a fury over his tests so he wanted his results to be as complete as possible. By now Salk had inoculated nearly two hundred people. Mass inoculation was still premature, however.

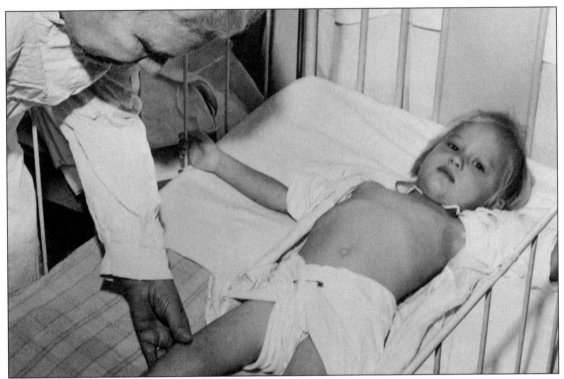

A nun attends to a young polio victim. Even as Salk hurried to perfect his vaccine, thousands of American children were stricken with polio.

TOSSING A BOMB

Salk knew, as did others, that they were not ready to inoculate tens of millions of America's children. Many unforeseen consequences could occur possibly causing thousands to become crippled or die. Some children might have an allergic reaction; some might have another disease that could nullify the vaccine; and an occasional dose of vaccine might become contaminated. No one was willing to take risks of that magnitude just yet—especially Salk.

Despite the logic of waiting to perform more trials, there was also the alternate reality for tens of thousands of Americans who continued to contract the disease because there was no vaccine. [In fact, the worst polio epidemic ever in America occurred during the summer of 1952.] Nearly sixty thousand people were paralyzed. Salk and all members of his team realized that whatever decision they made, they would affect the lives of millions, and they could not take unreasonable chances. Yet they also could not afford to be unreasonably cautious.

Salk decided to announce his secret trials at the next meeting with the full group of polio researchers in January 1953 in Hershey, Pennsylvania. Salk knew that his staff would need to be prepared for all possible objections that would arise at the meeting.

Although it continued to be important to maintain the secrecy of the tests, Francis, who knew of the experiments at the Watson and Polk facilities, could not resist confiding to a colleague regarding the upcoming Hershey meeting, "We're going to toss a bomb at you."[50]

It was a coincidence that Sabin had visited Salk's laboratory the day before the conference to see his laboratory and gather information about the research being performed there. Since both men would be attending the meeting in Hershey, the two rode the train there together. Although Sabin probed Salk about the status of his research, Salk said nothing about the news he was about to deliver.

The response to his news was just what Salk had anticipated. Opposition led by Sabin was swift and furious. All manner of concerns were raised, most of which were warranted. Adjuvants had been known in the past to have toxic effects; viruses grown in cultures of monkey tissue had at times caused organ failure; and the length of killed-virus immunity might last no longer than six months. Furthermore, what evidence did Salk have to prove that the killed-virus technique would produce higher levels of antibodies than levels produced by the live-virus technique?

Once the clamor subsided, the question regarding full field trials with large numbers of subjects arose. Salk was attempting to soften his enthusiasm for large field trials of one hundred thousand or more subjects by stating that even if he wanted to proceed, he did not have enough vaccine to get the job done. He had already hired Dr. Percival Bazeley, an Australian virologist with a reputation for producing large-scale volumes of vaccines, to solve the problem of how to create the gallons of vaccine that field trials would require.

To initiate field trials required the agreement of the leading figures in virology and immunology. The NFIP called a meeting of twenty leading researchers in February to discuss the matter. Noticeably missing were Sabin and others who had serious reservations about the safety of Salk's vaccine. As more and more scientists learned about Salk's test it was only a matter of time until the news would become public and cause an irrational demand to make the vaccine available immediately.

To counter the possibility of a public panic for a vaccine that had been tested on fewer than two hundred people and of which enough did not yet exist, it was decided that public statements would be made. Salk and others would publish their findings in medical journals to educate doctors about the status of polio research, and the NFIP would make a radio address to the nation.

Salk telephoned Sabin to consult with him regarding the text of the radio speech, but Sabin urged him not to make the speech. Sabin believed the public was being misled into thinking a vaccine was on the way, and he did not believe that Salk's vaccine had yet been proved safe and effective. In that regard, Sabin was correct, and Salk agreed. Salk, however, was confident that science and logic would eventually prove him correct.

On March 26, 1953, Basil O'Connor and Salk addressed the nation on radio to provide listeners with a summary of the status of the polio research. Salk was careful not only to point out some of the optimistic results of his research but also to warn that more work lay ahead and that no one should expect a vaccine immediately. In the March issue of the *Journal of the American Medical Association*, Salk published the results of his research and clinical tests. This two-pronged approach seemed to have accomplished the objectives of providing the facts and alerting the public and the medical community that a vaccine might be on the way.

On March 27 nearly every major newspaper carried the text of Salk's speech on the front page. His picture appeared in magazines the following week along with articles about his poliovirus research. Salk's easy and forthright manner of answering reporters' questions made him a hit with the press. They felt at ease with a great scientist who also had a pleasant manner and seemed to be a good human being. One reporter caught up in Salk's honest and simple manner was overheard to say, "He could sell me the Brooklyn

Sabin (left) and Salk at a polio conference. Despite Sabin's reservations, in March 1953 Salk made public the results of his secret trials.

Salk holds up two decanters containing his polio vaccine. Field trials required the production of hundreds of thousands of more polio vaccine doses.

Bridge."[51] Like it or not, Salk was becoming a celebrity.

At this point in time, Salk was clearly the man of the hour. In May a Gallup Poll reported that more Americans were aware of the upcoming field trials for Salk's polio vaccine than knew the full name of the president of the United States, Dwight David Eisenhower.

ENDLESS TINKERING

Field trials would require a large quantity of vaccine, far more than Salk and Bazeley could possibly produce. Production of hundreds of thousands of doses would require several large pharmaceutical laboratories. These laboratories would have to adhere rigidly to Salk's formula of ingredients and his directions concerning the sequence and circumstances of the actual production. Temperature control, filtration, measurement, blending, and sterilization all played into the vaccine production.

The various pharmaceutical laboratories were excited about the prospects of producing what might become one of the most important vaccines in the history of medicine. The problem, as the laboratories stated over and over again to Salk, was their need to get the vaccine formula and information about all of the conditions for production. Salk, however, always the perfectionist, was reluctant to comply with these requests until he was satisfied that he had the best possible formula.

Salk understood that the moment he released the formula to the pharmaceutical laboratories, it would be viewed as the finished product. Salk, however, wanted to continue to improve the vaccine. He insisted on exploring adjustments to the amount of the adjuvant, the formula for the formalin, the exposure time to ensure the poliovirus was killed but not rendered useless, and a seemingly endless list of other requirements.

Salk's friends and colleagues were becoming impatient with his insistence on perfection. The public already knew that field trials were soon to take place, and O'Connor and others were now under increasing pressure to produce the vaccine. Those who were putting pressure on Salk failed to realize that he was not just being a perfectionist. Salk certainly wanted to provide a vaccine that would be both safe and effective, but he also had a passion about the principle of killed-virus vaccines. He knew that live-virus vaccine advocates would label the killed-virus vaccine a failure if it showed any weakness or deficiency. He hoped to end the debate, once and for all, over the killed versus live virus dispute.

Dr. Thomas Rivers was becoming testy about the delays. Opponents of killed virus argued that no trial should be started until a live-virus vaccine became available. Salk wanted to be sure he had the best possible killed-virus vaccine. Rivers made it clear to everyone that it was time to stop the endless bickering and tinkering when he said:

> The first automobile was a far cry from today's cars but we did not go on walking while waiting for the 1954 models with all their improvements. So why let children continue to run the risk of polio when we have what might be the Model T [a popular car during the 1920s] of polio vaccines ready?[52]

Salk was still conducting laboratory tests when O'Connor told Salk that it was time to save lives. O'Connor believed they should begin the field trials by the end of the year on 388,800 American children. Although Salk objected, he agreed that it might be possible to meet that deadline.

FIELD TRIALS

Following many months of work on procedures for the production of large quantities of the vaccine, field trials were scheduled for the spring of 1954. It was just before the start of summer, which was always when the worst polio outbreaks occurred.

The person who agreed to oversee the trials was Salk's mentor Dr. Thomas Francis of the University of Michigan. Francis was well respected by everyone in the field and Salk trusted him to perform top-quality trials. Francis agreed to take the job even though he did not want to spend a year of his life away from his other research duties. He accepted, however, because he knew the significance of the trials. Francis would be the one to ensure that the trials were performed

The Electron Microscope and the Poliovirus

Salk and his colleagues would have given anything to be able to see the deadly culprit they were pursuing during the early years of their research in the late 1940s. The poliovirus, however, was so small that no one had a microscope powerful enough to see it.

Until the late 1930s, all microscopes were limited to magnifying only those substances that were larger than the wavelength of light. Smaller particles, such as viruses, could not be detected until the use of electron microscopes. Electrons have much shorter wavelengths than light waves. The highest magnification achievable with light microscopes is about two thousand times the actual size; electron microscopes are capable of magnifications of about one million times the actual size.

It was not until 1953 that electron microscopes improved to the point of being able to see an individual poliovirus. Although rudimentary at the time, the ability to see the poliovirus and watch it change when exposed to various chemicals and ultraviolet light revealed valuable secrets of its structure to polio researchers. On November 16, 1953, *Time* magazine carried this remarkable story documenting the first sighting of the virus:

"In all the years that medical researchers have been studying poliomyelitis, they have never seen the critter. Now two teams have isolated the virus, looked at it long and hard under the electron microscope, photographed it, and measured it. It turns out to be a spherical particle about one billionth of an inch in diameter. Magnified tens of thousands of times against a plastic screen, the virus particles look like tennis balls on an asphalt court. The reason for the long delay in completely isolating the virus was the difficulty of separating it from the substances in which it grows. Until recently, a relatively 'pure' preparation was only 1% virus and 99% 'gunk.'"

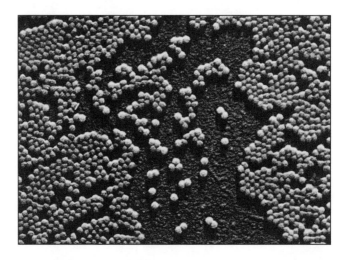

Until 1953 the poliovirus was too small to be seen even under a microscope.

according to rigid standards. He would also compile the results that would reveal to the nation whether or not the vaccine was safe and effective.

The purpose of field trials is to determine whether a vaccine is safe enough and effective enough to warrant its use for potentially hundreds of millions of people throughout the world. Should something go wrong during the field trials, or if nothing at all should happen, only a relatively small population would be affected. Field trials also require volunteer subjects who are warned of all possible adverse effects.

Most of the trials would be a "double-blind" test, meaning that roughly half of those inoculated would receive the Salk vaccine while the other half would receive a placebo, an inert substance that did not contain any vaccine. This was done to determine if the group that received the vaccine actually showed a lower rate of contracting polio than the group receiving the placebo. No one except Francis and his assistants would know which children received the vaccine injection and which the placebo. Not even the doctors administering the shots would know.

Pittsburgh elementary school students participate in polio vaccine field trials. The first field trials began in the spring of 1954.

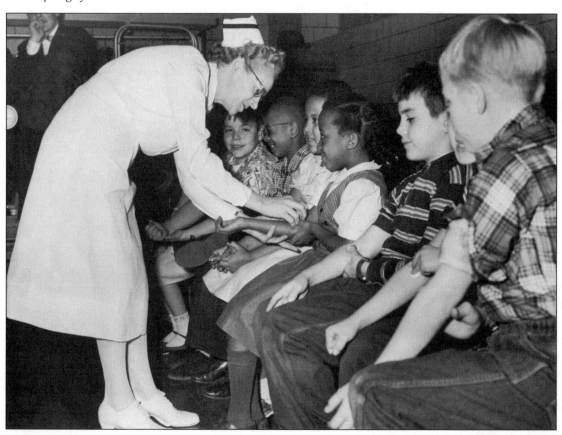

The field trials began April 26, 1954, with the inoculation of 642,360 elementary school children. Of those children, 441,131 received the vaccine and 201,229 received injections of the placebo. An additional several hundred thousand students acted as a control group, meaning they received no injections at all. The inoculations ended in early June for the students who lived in 217 counties across 44 states.

While Salk awaited the results of the field trials being carried out by Francis at the University of Michigan, he continued to modify and improve the potency of the vaccine formula. Salk was still working to improve the process for growing the virus in vitro as well as adjusting the time the virus was subjected to the formalin to ensure it was properly killed.

In early March 1955 the evaluation staff at the University of Michigan announced that it had completed its field trial analysis of the vaccine and would make its findings public sometime in April. Normally such announcements were made through scientific publications read only by members of the medical community. The NFIP and the University of Machigan realized, however, that the entire nation was awaiting the results and decided that this news would best be delivered publicly. On April 5 Francis announced that he had completed the final report and that a conference would be held at the university on April 12, exactly ten years after the death of the world's most famous polio victim, President Roosevelt.

The medical community and the nation awaited the results of the field trials. Unreliable speculation was rampant and ranged from total failure to total success. Salk himself, although confident that his approach to the vaccine had met all scientific requirements, looked forward to the announcement with some nervousness. Francis had not leaked any of the the results to him.

6 The Price of Success

Salk was not prepared for what was to occur in Ann Arbor on that April day. Although he assumed the results would be positive and that his vaccine would bring polio in America under control, he could not have predicted how it would adversely affect his life. Salk was about to learn that fame and success often cause unintended problems and hardships.

THE FRANCIS REPORT

The news media that descended on the university in Ann Arbor for the release of the results of the field trials was out of control. The swirl of reporters, photographers, and television cameras from throughout the nation and a few foreign countries on April 12, 1955, was unprecedented. Never before had television cameras been used along with print reporters and radio commentators to report a significant event. The frenzied atmosphere was in part due to a March 30 story that appeared in both the *New York World Telegraph* and the *Sun* newspapers. Both papers ran headline stories proclaiming that none of the children who had received the Salk vaccine had contracted polio or had become ill. The report

was not only premature, it was not true. Nonetheless, Salk and his family arrived in Ann Arbor to find that the news media was there to honor him.

Dr. Thomas Francis had planned to read a summary of the report at 10:20 A.M. followed by comments by Salk. Unfortunately, members of the overly aggressive press grabbed copies of everything and began transmitting their stories before Francis started his speech. The Associated Press telegraphed the following headline: "The Salk vaccine is safe, effective, and potent, it was officially announced today."[53]

At 10:20 A.M., Francis began a detailed discussion of the results. For the paralytic form of polio the vaccine had achieved 90 percent effectiveness against virus types II and III but only 60–70 percent against the more virile type I poliovirus. There had been one death of a vaccinated girl, which doctors later attributed to a tonsillectomy she had received following her inoculation. The results had not been as good as Salk had hoped but they were welcomed by the public. His colleagues were a bit more reserved. They recognized that the success rate for the type I virus, the most common type, also indicated a failure rate of 30–40 percent, a fact missed by the media and a fact that failed to dampen the enthusiasm displayed by the general public.

After Francis revealed the results, Salk stepped forth to the cheers and applause of the crowd. He gave a brief summary of the work and praised Francis and O'Connor for their assistance. He then went on to address the need for more research and the need to begin production of large quantities of his vaccine—which he called the Pitt vaccine after the University of Pittsburgh rather than the Salk vaccine. Finally, Salk made claims about the possibility in the near future of producing a polio vaccine that would be 100 percent effective.

Many colleagues felt that such a claim was premature and reckless at the time, considering the results of the type I vaccine. It was also statistically unlikely—no vaccine had ever achieved effectiveness above 95 percent. Later that day in Washington, D.C., the Secretary of Health, Education, and Welfare signed the order to license the Salk vaccine with the comment, "It's a great day. It is a wonderful day for the whole world."[54]

Dr. Thomas Francis announces the results of Salk's polio vaccine field trials. Although the public and press considered the trials a success, Salk had hoped for higher prevention rates.

An American Hero

However often Salk may have dreamed about becoming an American hero, he was not at all prepared to deal with what actually happened. Just forty years old, Salk found himself surrounded by people he did not know requesting his time to do things that he did not want to do. Salk would later recall the milestone in a conversation with Edward R. Murrow, the most famous reporter and television newscaster of the time:

"It Hurt"—Children's Letters to Dr. Salk

Immediately following the first authorized public inoculations, Salk received hundreds of letters from children expressing their appreciation for what he had done to protect them from polio. Most also took the opportunity to point out to Salk, in case he didn't know it, that the shots hurt. Some letters were written as a school assignment, but many others were from the heart. The post office managed to get all of them to Salk although an occasional envelope only had the name Dr. Jonas Salk, with no street address, city, or state.

The following three letters, which reside in the Jonas Salk Papers, Mandeville Special Collections Library, at the University of California, San Diego, exemplify the sorts of letters Salk received from appreciative children:

One seven-year-old wrote:

"Dear Dr. Saulk

You probably have never heard of me but I got you[r] shot today and I am ok. It hurt.
Thank you,
Fred"

A nine-year-old girl, although a bit confused as to what Salk had discovered, nonetheless understood that he had accomplished something special:

"Dear Dr. Salk,

I want to thank you for that wonderful experiment you discovered. I got my shot already and it only hurt a little. I think everyone should get it. I am sure glad God gave us men like you."
Thank you,
Peggy."

A ten-year-old young lady wrote:

"Dear Dr. Salk,

Although I am a girl of 10, I want to thank you for what you have given to the world. Your vaccine will save thousands and maybe millions of lives each year. You have made it so that 3 small hurts will prevent a great hurt. What I mean is that 3 small shots will prevent the great hurt of polio.
Thank you,
Ann.
P.S. Good luck."

President Dwight D. Eisenhower (center) presents Salk with a special presidential citation. Salk was overwhelmed by the praise and attention he garnered after the success of the vaccine's field trials.

I felt myself very much like someone in the eye of a hurricane, because all this swirling was going on around me. It was at that moment that everything changed. Edward R. Murrow, the journalist and newscaster, said to me that evening, "Young man, a great tragedy has just befallen you." I said, "What's that, Ed?" He said, "You've just lost your anonymity."[55]

Salk was inundated by requests for his time that he found utterly ridiculous. He rejected five requests to make a movie about his life and an offer to write a novel about his search for the poliovirus. He also laughed off offers to pay him to promote farm equipment, automobiles, and baby products. Everyone wanted to associate with the "Test Tube Doctor," the "Polio Man," or the "Guy in the White Lab Coat" as he was often called. When asked if he would endorse the breakfast cereal he ate each morning, he responded by asking the advertising agent why anyone could possibly care what he ate for breakfast. Such publicity stunts could easily be rejected but many other more serious requests for his time could not.

In late April, President Dwight D. Eisenhower invited Salk to the White House along with Basil O'Connor to receive a special presidential citation. Salk felt overwhelmed by all the attention he was receiving. He later confided to a reporter for the *New York Times* newspaper, "There we stood, my wife, three boys and myself, in the Rose Garden of the White House, while the President congratulated me. I thought to myself, 'What am I doing here?'"[56] The U.S. Congress later awarded Salk a congressional Gold Medal. During the halftime show for the Sugar Bowl football game that year, the marching band spelled out S-A-L-K on the football field. Everyone knew the name Dr. Salk.

Following the White House ceremony, many more honors were bestowed upon Salk in the United States as well as in Europe. Salk initially attended some of the ceremonies but soon was overwhelmed by the continuing gratitude expressed by so many countries, cities, and universities. He finally decided to accept awards but declined to attend the ceremonies.

Thousands of Americans sent Salk thank-you notes and telegrams. Hollywood stars such as Marlon Brando and Helen Hayes thanked him, and one of his mathematics teachers telegrammed him saying, "Congratulations Jonas—I knew you'd be successful."[57] Heartrending letters of appreciation came from children and parents thanking him for defeating the "Crippler," as polio was often called. Checks accompanied many letters as did individual dimes, which he deposited into a research account. Salk took the time to reply to many of the letters and contributions with a thank-you note.

To optimize his time, Salk believed it prudent to accept only a few opportunities to address the American public. Edward R. Murrow extended an invitation to Salk and Francis to appear on his television news show called *See It Now*. Murrow asked Salk at the end of the program who held the patent on the vaccine. Stunned by the question, Salk uttered the now famous answer, "Well, the people, I would say. There is no patent. Could you patent the sun?"[58] The fact that Salk was not making money directly from a patent on the vaccine greatly enhanced the public's admiration for his humanitarian selflessness.

A Gallup Poll asked Americans to name the most influential scientists of the time, and Jonas Salk placed second behind Dr. Robert Oppenheimer, the physicist credited with leading the team that developed the atom bomb at the end of World War II. Another poll asked Americans to name the greatest humanitarian of the world, and Salk tied with the brilliant German medical missionary and philosopher, Dr. Albert Schweitzer.

Salk's name filled the headlines of all major newspapers and magazines. *Newsweek* magazine on April 25, 1955, called Salk's discovery, "A quiet young man's magnificent victory."[59] The *New York Times Magazine* carried an article about Salk and his vaccine that managed to convey Salk's sense of having lost time for his research in the whirl of publicity:

> Salk is profoundly disturbed by the torrent of fame that has descended upon him. He is trying hard to keep himself and the scientific method with which he identifies from being sucked into a whirlpool of publicity, politics and pressure of various sorts. He talks continually about getting out of the lime-

light and back to his laboratory. "It's not a question of modesty," he says, "I want to keep up this vaccine job and get on to other things."[60]

Salk was eager to return to the laboratory to make good on his promise to increase the effectiveness of the vaccine. It would be years, however, until the modest "lab rat" in his white lab coat would be able to work quietly and without distraction in his laboratory.

Medical discoveries were usually announced in medical journals, not over national television. Many of Salk's colleagues were not happy about scientific research being put on public display. They saw the press conference as grandstanding.

Salk displays his presidential citation, one of the many honors he received.

CONTEMPT FROM COLLEAGUES

The release of the Francis Report in Ann Arbor on April 12, 1955, acknowledging the success of Salk's many years of diligent research on his vaccine also created a rift between Salk and many of his colleagues.

Great discoveries in the history of science are rarely the result of the efforts of just one person and Salk's discovery was no exception. He had many colleagues who contributed to his discoveries while working in his laboratory in Pittsburgh and in the laboratories of his competitors. Without their tireless work, the Salk vaccine could not have been produced.

Convention within the scientific community demanded that Salk open his comments that April day by generously handing out praise and appreciation for all who had contributed to his vaccine. The number of polio scientists who had made major contributions was lengthy—even Sabin had played a significant role.

Although he acknowledged the contributions of many others in his April 12 address, Salk actually named only a few key people including Francis and O'Connor. He did not list members of his research staff at Pittsburgh or the specific researchers who had made discoveries that assisted him in his search for a polio vaccine. Within the scientific community this was unforgivable. Salk's biographer Richard Carter made this poignant observation:

> Before the day's end, the gulf between him and his colleagues in polio research had widened impassibly. From their side they beheld a synthetic godling in custom-fitted halo, a smooth ambitious operator who had maneuvered his way to a kind of stardom that no true scientist would accept, much less seek.[61]

In addition to receiving criticism for what he did not say, Salk also received a stern reprimand for what he did say on April 12. Francis recalled being upset with Salk for the comment about achieving 100 percent effectiveness for his vaccine. "After Jonas was through talking, I went over to him, sore. 'What the hell did you say that for?' I said. 'You're in no position to claim 100 percent effectiveness. What's the matter with you?'"[62]

Barbs continued to be thrown at Salk from within the scientific community but in the eyes of the public, he was a hero. Salk refused to become bogged down by his critics because he felt he still had much work to do to improve the vaccine.

THE UNTHINKABLE

Shortly after the April 12 announcement several pharmaceutical laboratories began shipping the vaccine. By late April the shipments had reached cities all across the United States, and millions of elementary school children began lining up for shots.

Elation over the vaccine and its potential ended with a single phone call. Dr. James Shannon, assistant director of the National Institutes of Health, received that call just a few weeks after the shipments had arrived. Shannon later described the call:

> I was working over the weekend and I got a telephone call from Los Angeles, and this is eight or nine o'clock on Friday night. It was the Health Officer of

In Defense of Dr. Salk

Immediately following the April 12, 1955, announcement that Salk had discovered a safe and effective polio vaccine, he came under attack from colleagues for a variety of reasons. Criticism included his failure to acknowledge those who contributed to the success of the vaccine, the use of a risky killed virus, reckless endangerment by administering the vaccine to hundreds of thousands of children without proper testing, and callously seeking fame and fortune.

Few Americans, however, were interested in what they viewed as professional pettiness within the ranks of Salk's detractors. As far as they were concerned, a cure had been found and that was that. One such person, Annie Dillard, expressed the sentiment of most Americans when she defended Salk in a letter recorded in Jane Smith's book, Patenting the Sun:

"It was too quick, said medical colleagues nationwide: Salk had gone public without first publishing everything in the journals. He rushed out a killed-virus serum without waiting for a safe live-virus one, which would be better. Doctors walked out of professional meetings; some quit the foundation that funded the testing. Salk was after personal glory, they said. Salk was after money, they said. Salk was after big prizes.

Salk tested the serum on five thousand Pittsburgh school children, of whom I was three, because I kept changing elementary schools. Our parents, like ninety-five percent of all Pittsburgh parents, signed the consent form. Did the other mothers then bend over the desk in relief and sob? I don't know. But I don't suppose any of them gave much of a damn what Salk had been after."

the city of Los Angeles and he said they just had two reports of polio in some children who had been vaccinated nine days earlier. He wanted to know what should be done about it? [63]

The next day, more reports and phone calls crisscrossed the country with the same devastating news. As time went by, more cases were reported from several states, and by the end of the month, twenty-six vaccinated children had contracted polio. Basil O'Connor at the NFIP and the surgeon general of the United States began collecting data to determine what had gone wrong. Ultimately, 120 people contracted polio and 11 died.

Salk and his colleagues were devastated. The unthinkable had happened. Salk, who had moved forward with such confidence, pushed along by O'Connor and others, had given assurances that nothing would go wrong with the vaccine. Politicians were quick to attack everyone involved in the project as were newspaper columnists who demanded answers. Sabin and his supporters began an attack of "I told you so."

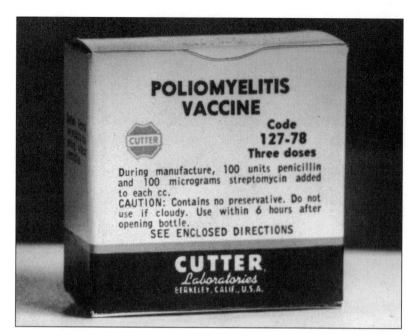

A box of Cutter polio vaccine. The first vaccines manufactured at Cutter Laboratories contained small amounts of live poliovirus and resulted in 120 people contracting the disease.

As the cases were analyzed, medical personnel recognized that all of the cases of polio were linked to only one of the several pharmaceutical companies that had been licensed to produce the vaccine, Cutter Laboratories in Berkeley, California. An analysis of the Cutter vaccine revealed that some of the poliovirus remained alive. Cutter Laboratories immediately suspended their operations, but Salk and others insisted that the remainder of the vaccines from the other companies continue to be administered.

Investigators from the National Institutes of Health descended on Cutter Laboratories. They found that Cutter technicians had not properly filtered the virus fluid. The resulting vaccine contained small amounts of live virus.

Directors at Cutter Laboratories vehemently argued that they had scrupulously adhered to the process defined by Salk.

They argued that Salk had not been precise enough when describing the filtration process. Salk, however, claimed that his procedure was precise, and that Cutter technicians had failed to execute his procedure properly. The government summoned Dr. Neal Nathanson and Alexander Langmuir to investigate. These two men recommended more stringent testing standards and later published their findings, in which they said in part:

> Vaccine produced and tested according to these revised standards has been carried out continuously since the spring of 1955. During the period between 1955 and 1961, over 400 million doses of poliomyelitis vaccine have been used without any evidence of inoculation poliomyelitis.[64]

Although the problem was quickly identified and corrected, famed San Francisco attorney Melvin Belli filed lawsuits on be-half of those infected. The courts ruled that Cutter had not acted negligently, but the company was found to have violated the warranty on the vaccine and was ordered to compensate the victims and their families.

THE PRICE OF FAME

Salk took the brunt of criticism for the Cutter incident. The nationally televised fanfare on April 12 announcing that the Salk vaccine was "safe, effective, and potent"

was still fresh in everyone's mind. The nation had come to recognize Dr. Salk from television and magazines and naturally associated him with the vaccine, calling it the "Salk vaccine" even though he opposed using his name for it. The American press had also dubbed Salk "The Polio Man" in appreciation for his pioneering work.

Now many leading polio researchers joined with the nonscientific community to chastise Salk and O'Connor. Renowned virologists, both friendly and antagonistic toward Salk and O'Connor, had warned them on many occasions that insufficient testing had been performed and that they

Attorney Melvin Belli represented polio victims in a lawsuit against Cutter Laboratories.

should wait until they could achieve a higher degree of safety for the vaccine. Sabin and several other virologists and immunologists voiced their opinion that a reliable vaccine was still many years in the future and that only a live-virus vaccine would ever be successful.

The joy that had resonated across America earlier that month ended only two weeks later when the Cutter problem was identified. As a consequence of Salk's fame, Americans felt deceived by him, the NFIP, and the government as a whole. In spite of the devastating news, Salk never lost confidence in his vaccine while learning that fame can demand a high price. Lawrence J. Peterson, the Idaho state health director, spoke for many Americans when he said, "We have lost confidence in the Salk vaccine."[65] Despite the criticism, once the tragedy had been corrected, Salk confided to reporter Jane Krieger:

THE WISDOM OF DR. SALK

As the years passed by, Salk made many careful observations about people and how they lived their lives by noting both their successes and their failures. He developed a repertoire of aphorisms to help people understand what he believed to be important lessons in life. The following are a few of his favorite sayings provided by Walter Eckhart and Kathleen Murray:

On experimentation:
We must keep an open mind and realize that no experiment, well conceived, ever fails. Every experience in life, as well as in science, teaches us something. We did not arrive at the stage we are at today by guessing—but rather by carefully calculated steps.

On failure:
We only fail when we quit too soon.

On opportunity:
Just because you don't get what you want doesn't make the situation a tragedy. It means you have an opportunity to do something different that may be even better.

On the value of enemies:
Your enemies help you define your position.

On aspirations:
Do what makes your heart leap.

On doing your best:
Optimize, don't compromise.

On positive thoughts:
Accentuate the positive and ignore the negative.

On perfection:
Any task worth doing is worth doing well.

Children line up outside an elementary school to receive Salk's polio vaccine. Although schools and public health offices offered the vaccine for free, some private doctors charged exorbitant fees to administer it.

You find yourself projected into a set of circumstances for which neither your training nor your talents have prepared you. It's very difficult in some respects, but it's a transitory thing and you wait till it blows over. Eventually people will start thinking, "That poor guy," and leave me alone. Then I'll be able to get back to my laboratory.[66]

BACK TO THE LABORATORY

Salk believed that once the Cutter Laboratories problem was rectified he would be able to return to his laboratory. This did not happen. The successful resolution of the Cutter issue did not mean that the remaining unvaccinated children suddenly received their inoculations. Some civic leaders and politicians began referring to children as guinea pigs, causing many parents to hesitate over immunizing their children.

Salk realized he had to act. In June 1956 he wrote letters to all of the medical societies urging doctors to promote vaccinations in all public schools. When he heard that some doctors were charging exorbitant amounts of money to administer his vaccine in their private offices, he publicly chastised those doctors. He reminded the public that they could get the same vaccine free at schools and public health offices.

Salk's time was further taken up by demands from the media and others. Presidents, kings, and other heads of state invited Salk to their countries, and refusing such invitations would have been considered an insult. Following a few trips to Europe, Salk tired of the routine and finally found diplomatic ways to decline any further European trips so that he could return to his work.

Salk finally did manage to return to his laboratory. By 1960 he had begun to evaluate how long immunity lasted in children who received commercially produced vaccine. Opinions varied from one year to a lifetime. Salk's initial finding showed that antibody levels in the earliest vaccine recipients persisted for at least five years. This was encouraging news.

Though more study was needed, Salk's work represented an enormous triumph. In 1952, the worst year for polio infection in America, 57,740 cases were recorded. In 1956, the year following the first inoculations, the number dropped to 15,463. In 1957 it fell dramatically to 5,485, and by 1962 the number was at 910. In 1994 the National Institutes of Health announced that no new cases of naturally occurring polio were being reported.

With the bulk of his work on the polio vaccine behind him, Salk looked forward to the 1960s as a time to move on to a new medical agenda. Salk was now ready to turn his scientific curiosity to new challenges.

Chapter
7 Blueprint for Unconventional Creativity

As the decade of the 1960s began, Dr. Jonas Salk entered a new stage in his thinking that would occupy him for the remainder of his life. He began to express the idea that the solutions for future problems would arise from combining knowledge of science, the

Physicist Robert Oppenheimer and others helped Salk outline a unique intellectual center.

arts, and philosophy. He believed that many good minds with many different points of view would produce the clearest vision of where the human species was going and how to solve the many problems that lay on the path to the future.

To investigate his ideas more fully, Salk sought out people such as Robert Oppenheimer and Leo Szilard, both renowned physicists. Salk began to sketch the outlines for an intellectual center unlike any existing university or research institute. Salk would continue to work as a medical research scientist on new projects, but his approach would be as unorthodox as his killed-virus polio vaccine.

A TIME FOR TRANSITION

The board of directors at the University of Pittsburgh Medical School renamed the hospital where Salk performed his polio research "Salk Hall" to honor their most famous scientist and to encourage him to remain on the staff to investigate a cure for cancer. The university also offered Salk a position to head an experimental medical staff but the idea of working as an administrator failed to interest him. He knew that such a position would only help to keep him from the laboratory work he longed for.

Salk had endured a mentally and physically exhausting period since he began his assault on polio in 1947. Many successful scientists who had worked sixteen-hour days for years with very few vacations tended to end their careers pursuing more leisurely interests than lab research. Some delivered lectures to the admiring public while others functioned as senior-level consultants to young researchers—few returned to the confines of a laboratory for a second major assault on a disease. Salk, however, was still quite young and had no interest in retirement—as he made clear in an interview with Richard Carter: "I wanted an unstructured situation where almost anything would be possible. The world was open. Knowledge was expanding. I wanted to be in the thick of things. I could not see myself voluntarily withdrawing to administration and lectureships at this stage of life."[67]

Salk continued to discuss with several of his closest colleagues and friends the idea about creating an institute that would function unlike universities or research companies. The institute would be a community of scholars who would work at the institute to solve medical problems without the interferences that so often plague universities and privately owned research facilities. In addition, Salk believed that philosophers and artists working at the institute might bring insights that doctors who were overly emerged in their work might not see.

Salk's years of work on both influenza and polio had led him to understand that the relationship between viruses, cells, human organs, and finally human beings was far too complex to be understood by one or two scientific departments. An institute would be the ideal setting for the many disparate branches of science to focus on the resolution of common problems. Many unorthodox points of view, Salk reasoned, might generate the best solutions.

THE SALK INSTITUTE

Establishing Salk's revolutionary institute required money, a location, and a name. Basil O'Connor and the March of Dimes pledged $15 million, which was enough money in 1959 for Salk to select a site in the coastal San Diego community of La Jolla, California. The twenty-six-acre site for the institute, situated on a bluff directly above the sandy southern California beaches below, could scarcely have been more beautiful. The site had the additional intellectual and cultural attraction of being located adjacent to the Scripps Institution of Oceanography and the future San Diego campus of the University of California.

The acreage was surrounded by a rare and distinctive species of pine tree, the Torrey pine, and Salk chose to name the new institute the Torrey Pines Institute of Biological Studies. O'Connor, however, overruled him insisting that the institute be called the Salk Institute of Biological Studies in order to identify it with Salk, honor his work, and motivate philanthropists and corporations to donate money.

Salk worked with the architect, Louis Kahn, to design the institute's buildings, making many suggestions for change before their construction. In 1960 the Salk

BUILDING THE SALK INSTITUTE

The building and planning of the Salk Institute overlooking the Pacific Ocean was one of Salk's most cherished achievements. Salk worked closely with architect Louis Kahn to create a futuristic campus of free-flowing laboratories, offices, conference rooms, quiet meditative areas, and libraries that would facilitate creative ideas and thought. Chalkboards were even installed in the exterior walls, inviting creative expression while the staff took a breath of fresh air.

The Salk Institute remains one of the most famous architectural landmarks in San Diego County. Kahn designed two parallel laboratories intersecting with the Pacific's horizon, each 65 feet wide by 245 feet long, encircled by a perimeter corridor. Between the two laboratory buildings is a stark white travertine courtyard with a simple narrow water channel that cuts the entire length and draws the observer's eye to the seemingly infinite blue Pacific in the distance. The water channel leads to a waterfall at the west end that is surrounded by outdoor dining tables for the staff. According to Paul Heyer, author of *American Architecture: Ideas and Ideologies in the Late Twentieth Century,* "The central court, as a . . . space of shimmering blue water, a band pointing toward the ocean epitomizing what human endeavor can accomplish." To Salk, the institute might soon become the Athens of the West.

Salk's involvement in the design was significant enough to prompt the American Institute of Architects to elect him to their board of directors. Kathleen Murray stressed

Salk's love of the buildings by pointing out in an interview, "He was involved in all facets of design and construction right down to the color and texture of the concrete walls and the shape and color of the exposed ends of the steel form-ties that bind the concrete blocks." According to Murray, "A day didn't pass that Jonas didn't appreciate the institute, there was a special sweetness with which he loved it."

The courtyard of the Salk Institute reflects Salk's vision for the site.

Institute was officially founded. The dedication ceremony took place in 1963 even though the institute buildings were only partially completed.

THE COMMUNITY OF SCHOLARS

The community of diverse intellectuals that Salk envisioned as the future of science was fast becoming a reality. At the time of the dedication ceremony Salk had already managed to attract forty world-renowned thinkers including Francis Crick, Nobel Prize winner for his shared discovery of the molecular structure of the deoxyribonucleic acid (DNA) molecule; C.P. Snow, a British scientist and man of literature; Jacques Monod, Nobel Prize winner in medicine; Leo Szilard, theoretical and nuclear physicist; Melvin Cohn, biophysicist and chemist; and Jacob Bronowski, mathematician, philosopher, and writer. The presence of Jacob Bronowski, internationally known for his exceptional ability to communicate with scientists, poets, and philosophers, was a tremendous boost for Salk's dream.

Bronowski accepted an invitation to write a book and present a television series titled *The Ascent of Man*, which was filmed between July 1971 and December

Nuclear physicist Leo Szilard was just one of the intellectuals who worked at the Salk Institute in California.

THE POLIO VACCINE TODAY

Although there have been no new cases of naturally occurring polio in the United States in more than twenty years, children today continue to receive polio vaccinations. Since polio is still diagnosed in other parts of the world, doctors reason that the virus could reemerge in America. Thus, a global effort to eliminate the disease will continue until polio is completely eradicated worldwide.

Both Salk's inactivated polio vaccine (IPV), developed in 1955, and Sabin's oral polio vaccine (OPV), developed in early 1960s, are effective in providing immunity against polio. In recent years, OPV has been the form most commonly used because, according to the CDC, it is better at keeping the disease from spreading to other people. However, OPV, which contains a small amount of weakened but still live virus, can very rarely cause people to get sick. In fact, OPV causes polio in roughly one in 2.4 million people.

Because the risk of polio is extremely low in the United States, in 1999 the Advisory Committee for Immunization Practices suggested that using OPV was no longer worth the slight risk associated with it. The committee recommended that by January 2001 all children receive IPV rather than OPV since IPV does not contain any live polio virus. As a result, the standard practice for childhood polio vaccination consists of four doses of IPV. One dose is given at two months of age, the next at four months, the next at six to eighteen months, and the last at four to six years.

1972. In this book and subsequent television series, Bronowski traced the development of science as an expression of the characteristics that make human beings preeminent among animals. Bronowski was the best known of the few great thinkers who generated inspiration by bridging the hard sciences, the soft sciences, and the arts.

In addition to resident scholars, Salk wanted to invite artists to set up studios at the institute to paint and sculpt, and he wanted to build an auditorium for musicians to perform original works as well as the classics. Salk was convinced that intellectual diversity would facilitate an uncommon exchange of unorthodox ideas among the scientists and artists for the betterment of all disciplines. As Salk explained the synthesis, "We're going to have to rely on artists as well as scientists for the solutions we need."[68]

Although everyone agreed that the institute provided a unique environment for the exchange of unusual points of view, the idea of blending art and science failed to take hold. Scientists from different fields interacted and novel approaches to solving scientific questions arose, but except for Bronowski's project no formal programs were established.

A New Personal Life

By the early 1970s, Salk realized he would have to defer his grand experiment. Although he never lost confidence in its potential, he saw that it was simply ahead of its time. Undaunted by the direction his community of scholars had taken, knowing that the institute had become a major center of biomedical research, Salk pondered his future. The institute had consumed most of Salk's time, although a little of it had been spent in his lab. As head of the institute, Salk had been caught in the trap of endless meetings, fundraisers, and travel to conferences around the world to attract faculty and to answer questions about his institute. Even the everyday functioning of the institute had begun to take up much of his time.

The pressure of Salk's routine also had placed stress on his wife, Donna. She had single-handedly raised their three children during his years of sixteen-hour days at the lab. Now she was expected to attend all of the fundraising and social functions for her husband's institute. Jonas and Donna decided to go their separate ways in 1968 after twenty-eight years of marriage.

In 1970 Salk met the French painter Françoise Gilot at a gathering of friends and later gave her a tour of his institute. The two struck up an immediate friendship that led to their marriage that same year. Although the two had very different intellectual interests, they nonetheless drew energy and enthusiasm for their work from each other's creative pursuits. According to Salk's personal administrative assistant, Kathleen Murray, "Dr. Salk often said of his relationship with his wife,

Salk and his second wife, Françoise Gilot, pose in front of one of her paintings.

'She's a scientific artist and I'm an artistic scientist.'" [69]

Searching the Philosophical Horizon

With his new wife, Salk continued to search for a new path to follow in his career. He searched for ideas that would express his philosophical views on science and humanity. The decade of the 1960s had been a time to plan, build, and launch the Salk Institute; the 1970s would be the decade to turn his thoughts to a variety of philosophical topics such as the nature of creativity, the continuing evolution of humanity, population control, science and humanity, world peace, and how humanity can achieve its highest potential.

Salk published four books during the 1970s, each of which addressed his thoughts on a broad range of topics. His work in medicine and his later friendships with scholars representing all intellectual disciplines began to shape Salk's global view of the future of humankind.

In Salk's first book, *Man Unfolding,* he discusses the emergence and development of the human mind in terms of biological evolution and development. Salk explains his view that the orderly design of the most elemental particles of life led to the orderly formation of the human brain. He then discusses the leap that the physical brain makes to spiritual awareness and its ability to think on higher orders than the brains of other animals. Throughout the book, Salk points to what he believes to be a reasoned purpose behind evolution.

In *The Survival of the Wisest,* Salk expresses his view that humankind is entering a new era, which he calls Epoch B. During this era, human consciousness will prevail to enable people to use their imaginations and intellects to solve the many challenges facing the world in modern times. Salk makes the argument that learning to collectively act

SALK THE EVOLUTIONIST

Following Salk's pinnacle discovery of the polio vaccine, he worked on many other diseases including cancer, multiple sclerosis, and AIDS. Although all of these research efforts called upon his intellect as a biologist, virologist, and immunologist, perhaps most apparent during his latter years was his intellect as an evolutionist.

The book Salk most enjoyed discussing with friends was his *Survival of the Wisest.* Salk built his theories upon the thinking of the great British naturalist Charles Darwin and his book, *The Origin of Species,* in which Darwin set forth his theory of biological evolution. Although he built his ideas on Darwin's, Salk was quick to point out that his theories of evolution are very different. Darwin's ideas focused on the physical biological evolution of animals whereas Salk's ideas focus on the *metabiological* evolution of consciousness and the mind.

In an interview with Peter Stoler in March 1993 that appeared in *Psychology Today,* Salk explains, "In metabiological evolution, ideas determine the nature, characteristics, and behavior of a metabiological cell—an individual—or the metabiological organism—the society. The development, some 10,000 years ago, of agriculture would be a key example of a metabiological change. Another would be the printing press. The invention of tools, an expression of the capacity of the human mind, is another example of metabiological change. I would also include the development of ideas. Darwin's concept of evolution, Newton's celestial mechanics, Einstein's attempts at developing a unified field theory. Metabiological evolution is anything that results in an increase in consciousness."

wisely is crucial for arriving at a good quality of life on the planet and for preserving the planet. Salk's hypothesis is that humans can control evolution through wise choices and a sense of responsibility toward future generations. Wise choices leading to controlled evolution include the development of agriculture, the invention of tools, and mass communication. Throughout the book Salk maintains optimism about the future of humans through continued wise evolution but also warns that if wisdom is not pursued, large-scale tragedy may be the price.

In his book, *Anatomy of Reality: Merging of Intuition and Reason,* Salk writes about the evolution of the biosphere through the use of both intuition and reason. He believes strongly that intuition points people in the direction they should follow, and that reason then takes over to solve the problems that intuition points them to. Aside from his belief that the application of both intuition and reason is a fruitful approach to problem solving, Salk also contends that more people must learn to think independently in order to find those insights that will be of value in the evolutionary process.

Salk's last book, *World Population and Human Values: A New Reality,* was coauthored with his son Jonathan. The two men explore the problems of global overpopulation and trace changes in human attitudes to developments in population. The Salks predict that world population will rise sharply but will be forced to stabilize due to depletion of natural resources, pollution, and overcrowding in urban centers. They also explain that resolving conflicts over human values, attitudes, and behavior eventually will bring about improvements in health, well-being, and satisfaction with life.

THE 1980s

Salk sensed that although many of his colleagues revered him as the great sage of the institute as well as mentor to many younger scientists, others believed it was time for new ideas to take form in his laboratory. A few of his colleagues also were at odds with his philosophical ideas and believed they were inappropriate at a medical research institute where "hard" science was practiced. Salk once observed, "I couldn't possibly have become a member of this Institute, you know, if I hadn't organized it myself."[70]

An agreement had been made when the institute was founded that all scientists would vacate their laboratories on their seventieth birthday. In 1984, at the age of seventy, Salk emptied his laboratory at the institute to make way for younger scientists and new experiments that expressed their interests. Although he vacated his laboratory, he continued to maintain an office at the institute and went there nearly every day he was in town, for the rest of his life.

AIDS RESEARCH

During the years Jonas Salk was writing his books, a new epidemic called the Acquired Immune Deficiency Syndrome (AIDS) struck the world. It was a disease that was becoming more threatening than the polio epidemics of the early and mid-twentieth century. As the AIDS epidemic spread, pio-

In 1984 Salk gave up his laboratory at the institute, making room for a new generation of scientists.

neering researchers had just begun to understand what caused the disease and how it was transmitted. Salk, who had had to retire from his laboratory at the Salk Institute, believed it was time for him to get involved with the disease that was now killing tens of thousands of people annually.

In April 1987 Salk reemerged to join with other scientists and investors and establish a new company in the coastal community of Carlsbad, just fifteen miles north of the Salk Institute in La Jolla. The charter of the new company, named the Immune Response Company, was to take the lead in basic research to find ways of preventing disease caused by the Human Immunodeficiency Virus (HIV). The hope was that

Salk's unconventional approach would conquer this virus associated with AIDS as it had conquered the poliovirus. When the company announced that the man who had conquered polio had started a company to search for an AIDS vaccine, the newspapers and television news stations flashed the news throughout the world. The idea of the Polio Man working on an AIDS vaccine ignited hope and enthusiasm for those devastated by the disease. By this time, an estimated nine million people had contracted AIDS and there was no cure on the horizon. Even the most basic understanding of the disease had not yet been established. As with polio during the 1940s, basic laboratory research was needed.

Salk took the same unconventional approach toward HIV that he had taken toward the poliovirus. Unlike traditional vaccines, which are designed to prevent infection, Salk's approach was to create a killed-virus vaccine to inoculate people who were already infected with the virus. Once every three months, they would receive a shot of vaccine that would supposedly boost their defenseless immune system and decrease the amount of virus circulating in their blood.

Other AIDS researchers, aware of Salk's earlier success with the killed-virus, scoffed at his approach because HIV is far more complex than the poliovirus. Unlike the three types of the poliovirus, twenty-five HIV types were known and could unpredictably mutate. As had been the case forty years earlier, the killed-virus approach was dismissed by virtually all other researchers as too dangerous because it might accelerate rather than slow down the onset of the disease.

Despite criticism, Salk moved forward. In 1992 Salk arrived at what he believed to be a revolutionary understanding about the direction of AIDS research. While studying a medical journal about the leprosy virus, which is very different from HIV yet has a few similarities, Salk became convinced that the human body could fight the virus more effectively by producing T-cells (the components in blood that directly attack foreign substances in the body) than by producing antibodies. While attending the eighth annual AIDS conference in Amsterdam that same year, he expressed this unorthodox view. As had been the case many years earlier, the majority of

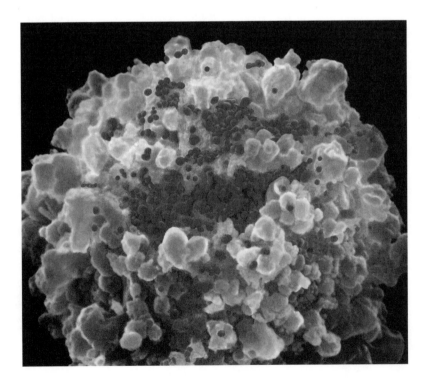

A T-cell infected with HIV. Salk's ideas about an HIV/AIDS vaccine were as unconventional as his poliovirus theory had been forty years earlier.

his colleagues thought his idea was ridiculous.

Although most researchers rejected Salk's view, his address did have the positive result of stimulating new discussions, controversies, and ideas about HIV. This outcome in itself gave value to Salk's research as well as his willingness to confront the medical community one more time with his unorthodox ideas. Unbeknownst to everyone including Dr. Salk, this would be the last time.

In June 1995 Jonas Salk died before he or anyone else was able to find a cure for AIDS. Nonetheless, his contributions set in motion a new debate about the AIDS virus and the most expeditious approach to fighting this worldwide epidemic. Earlier in 1990, Anthony Fauci, director of the National Institute of Allergy and Infectious Diseases complimented Salk's involvement in AIDS research with this remark: "Jonas Salk could rest on his laurels if he wanted to, but 35 years later [following the polio vaccine] he's still knee-deep in the trenches trying to make a contribution for another very devastating disease."[71]

Following the Path to the End

When Jonas Salk passed away at the age of eighty, he was eulogized for his heroic contribution in eliminating one of the world's worst childhood diseases. Obituaries in every major newspaper and magazine retold the story of the man in the white laboratory coat who developed a vaccine to prevent polio.

While proud of his accomplishments, during his life Salk had also been aware of the alienation that had developed between him and many of his polio colleagues. As for the criticism leveled against him for using the ideas of others without proper acknowledgment, he is remembered for this analogy to nature:

> What comes to mind now, is what I call the "sea gull syndrome." When I walk on the beach, I see a sea gull, going out and getting a fish or a piece of bread on the beach. And the others go after him rather than go get their own. And so I see sometimes that if someone does something and gets credit for it, there is this tendency to have this competitive response.[72]

Regardless of the politics surrounding the polio vaccine, everyone agrees that Salk never quit—he followed the path to the end. Salk built his success on the very criticism that he received. Had he not held fast to his convictions that the killed-virus technique was the right path to follow, he might have failed. Had he not persevered in spite of his critics, he might have failed. By moving forward with the confidence that hard work and clear logic would lead to success, Dr. Salk saved thousands of lives.

Following his great contribution, Salk continued to influence people through his writings about the future role of humanity and the future of the earth. Although he never returned to his legendary sixteen-hour workdays, he nonetheless divided his time between projects in the laboratory and his many other projects for the betterment of humanity. Walter Eckhart explained the important role Salk fulfilled outside the laboratory by saying, "Jonas enjoyed visiting other countries to express his concern for the well-being of children and to help promote world peace. Even when he was absent from the Institute, he kept in touch with what was going on in the labs there."[73]

To those who knew Salk during the second half of his life, he was a man who had always asked tough questions that had tough answers. He was a man willing to take chances, a man who thought in unconventional terms, a spiritual man with a deep concern about the future of the earth and those living on it.

Much of Salk's greatest work, though not as well publicized as his earlier triumphs, was performed late in life, yet it concerned the future. He urged people to be good ancestors and foresaw a time when suffering would be uncommon and human fulfillment the norm. He maintained that evolution could be shaped and that wise decisions would allow humankind collectively to find that fulfillment. Walter Eckhart summarized Salk's philosophical outlook this way: "Jonas was a visionary. He was unusually insightful and ahead of his time with regard to large subjects such as human nature, evolution, and the future of the planet."[74]

Salk was also a perpetual optimist. A few days before he passed away he had been in the hospital for a cardiac irregularity. While in the hospital his work and correspondence had piled up on his desk. The day after his release from the hospital he entered his office at the Salk Institute and

Throughout his lifetime, Salk remained an innovator, a visionary, and an optimist.

greeted Kathleen Murray with the last words she would ever hear from him: "We're going to come back stronger than ever—you just wait and see. We're going to get through all of this stuff just fine."[75]

Notes

Introduction: The Forgotten Epidemic

1. Quoted in Judith Bustamante and Lauren Eve Pomerantz, "To Catch a Killer: The Search for the Vaccine to Prevent Poliomyelitis," NBCI, http://members.nbci.com/poliostory/salk.html.

Chapter 1: Preparing for Success

2. Richard Carter, *Breakthrough: The Saga of Jonas Salk*. New York: Trident Press, 1966, p. 29.

3. Quoted in "Jonas Salk, M.D. Developer of Polio Vaccine," May 16, 1991, available from The American Gallery of Achievement, www.achievement.org/autodoc/page/sal0bio-1.

4. Quoted in "Jonas Salk, M.D. Developer of Polio Vaccine."

5. Quoted in "Jonas Salk, M.D. Developer of Polio Vaccine."

6. Quoted in "Jonas Salk, M.D. Developer of Polio Vaccine."

7. Quoted in John Rowland, *The Polio Man: The Story of Jonas Salk*. New York: Roy Publishers, 1960, p. 14.

8. Quoted in Carter, *Breakthrough,* p. 30.

9. Quoted in Carter, *Breakthrough,* p. 30.

10. Quoted in "Jonas Salk, M.D. Developer of Polio Vaccine."

11. Quoted in Carter, *Breakthrough,* p. 31.

12. Quoted in Bill Moyers, *A World of Ideas II: Public Opinions from Private Citizens*. New York: Doubleday, 1990, p. 236.

13. Dr. Walter Eckhart, interview with author, Salk Institute, La Jolla, California, August 22, 2001.

14. Quoted in "Jonas Salk, M.D. Developer of Polio Vaccine."

15. Quoted in Greer Williams, *Virus Hunters*. New York: Knopf, 1959, p. 273.

Chapter 2: Becoming a Scientist

16. Quoted in Carter, *Breakthrough*, pp. 37–38.

17. Jane Smith, *Patenting the Sun: Polio and the Salk Vaccine*. New York: William Morrow, 1990, p. 176.

18. Quoted in "Jonas Salk, M.D. Developer of Polio Vaccine."

19. Quoted in "Jonas Salk, M.D. Developer of Polio Vaccine."

20. Quoted in "Jonas Salk, M.D. Developer of Polio Vaccine."

21. Quoted in Carter, *Breakthrough*, p. 46.

22. Quoted in Carter, *Breakthrough*, p. 48.

23. Quoted in Carter, *Breakthrough*, p. 48.

24. Quoted in Carter, *Breakthrough*, p. 48.

25. Quoted in Carter, *Breakthrough*, p. 51.

26. Quoted in Carter, *Breakthrough*, p. 51.

27. Quoted in Carter, *Breakthrough*, p. 51.

Chapter 3: The Opportunity Others Did Not See

28. Quoted in Carter, *Breakthrough*, p. 53.

29. Quoted in "Jonas Salk, M.D. Developer of Polio Vaccine."

30. Quoted in Carter, *Breakthrough*, p. 55.

31. Quoted in "Jonas Salk, M.D. Developer of Polio Vaccine."

32. Quoted in Carter, *Breakthrough*, p. 63.

33. Quoted in Carter, *Breakthrough*, p. 62.

34. Quoted in Carter, *Breakthrough*, p. 66.

35. Quoted in "Jonas Salk, M.D. Developer of Polio Vaccine."

36. Quoted in Carter, *Breakthrough*, p. 81.

37. Quoted in Carter, *Breakthrough*, p. 82.

38. John Rodman Paul, *A History of Poliomyelitis*. New Haven: Yale University Press, 1971, p. 233.

39. Smith, *Patenting the Sun*, pp. 115–16.

Chapter 4: Building with the Help of Others

40. Quoted in Greer Williams, *Virus Hunters*, p. 270.

41. Quoted in Carter, *Breakthrough*, p. 120.

42. Quoted in Carter, *Breakthrough*, p. 114.

43. Dr. Walter Eckhart, interview with author, Salk Institute, La Jolla, California, August 22, 2001.

44. Quoted in Carter, *Breakthrough*, p. 126.

45. Quoted in Carter, *Breakthrough*, p. 129.

Chapter 5: A Shot in the Arm

46. Quoted in Carter, *Breakthrough*, p. 130.

47. Quoted in Carter, *Breakthrough*, p. 139.

48. Quoted in Carter, *Breakthrough*, p. 140.

49. Quoted in Marilyn Chase, "AIDS Scientist's Self-Inoculation Sparks Debate," *Wall Street Journal*, March 19, 1987.

50. Quoted in Carter, *Breakthrough*, p. 142.

51. Quoted in Williams, *Virus Hunters*, p. 292.

52. Quoted in Smith, *Patenting the Sun*, p. 219.

Chapter 6: The Price of Success

53. Quoted in Williams, *Virus Hunters*, p. 315.

54. Quoted in Williams, *Virus Hunters*, p. 320.

55. Quoted in "Jonas Salk, M.D. Developer of Polio Vaccine."

56. Quoted in June Krieger, "What Price Fame to Dr. Salk," *New York Times Magazine*, July 17, 1955, pp. 6–8.

57. Contained within the Jonas Salk Papers, Mandeville Special Collections Library, the University of California, San Diego.

58. Quoted in Carter, *Breakthrough*, p. 284.

59. *Newsweek*, "A Quiet Young Man's Magnificent Victory," April 25, 1955, p. 66–67.

60. Krieger, "What Price Fame to Dr. Salk," pp. 6–8.

61. Carter, *Breakthrough*, p. 269.

62. Quoted in Carter, *Breakthrough*, p. 281.

63. Quoted in Edward Shorter, *The Health Century*. New York: Doubleday, 1987, p. 67.

64. Neal Nathanson and Alexander Langmuir, "The Cutter Incident: Part I," *American Journal of Hygiene*, vol. 78, July 1963, p. 24.

65. Quoted in Williams, *Virus Hunters*, p. 340.

66. Quoted in Carter, *Breakthrough*, p. 335.

Chapter 7: Blueprint for Unconventional Creativity

67. Quoted in Carter, *Breakthrough*, p. 395.

68. Quoted in Peter Stoler, "A Conversation with Jonas Salk," *Psychology Today*, March 1983, p. 56.

69. Kathleen Murray, interview with author at the Salk Institute, September 5, 2001.

70. Quoted in Carter, *Breakthrough*, p. 413.

71. Quoted in Fauci, "Still in the Trenches: Jonas Salk," *U.S. News & World Report*, July 9, 1990, p. 52.

Epilogue: Following the Path to the End

72. Quoted in "Jonas Salk, M.D. Developer of Polio Vaccine."

73. Dr. Walter Eckhart, interview with author, August 22, 2001.

74. Eckhart, interview with author, August 22, 2001.

75. Kathleen Murray, interview with author, September 5, 2001.

For Further Reading

John Bankston, *Jonas Salk and the Polio Vaccine*, Bear, DE: Mitchell Lane, 2001. This biography highlights Salk's life and the medical work he conducted in his search for a successful polio vaccine. It includes discussion of Salk's struggles against anti-Semitism, the importance of President Franklin Delano Roosevelt in the polio campaign, and Salk's rivalry with Dr. Albert Sabin.

Stephanie Sammartino McPherson, *Jonas Salk: Conquering Polio*, Minneapolis, MN: Lerner, 2001. This biography of Jonas Salk focuses primarily on his personality and desire to conquer polio. Although it includes medical discussion where appropriate, the book concentrates on Salk's contribution as a human being.

Bill Moyers, *A World of Ideas II: Public Opinions from Private Citizens*. New York: Doubleday, 1990. This book is the result of a series of interviews that Bill Moyers conducted with twenty-nine famous creative people, including Jonas Salk. The interviews were originally released for television and later published in his book.

John Rowland, *The Polio Man: The Story of Jonas Salk*. New York: Roy Publishers, 1960. This work provides a good general discussion of Salk and his discovery of the polio vaccine. It does not, however, cover any of Salk's later life.

Victoria Sherrow. *Jonas Salk*, New York: Facts On File, 1993. This biography provides a complete and clear discussion of the work performed by Salk including much of his work at the Salk Institute toward the end of his life. Includes excellent discussions of the medical challenges that polio researchers overcame in discovering a successful polio vaccine.

Edward Shorter, *The Health Century*. New York: Doubleday, 1987. Shorter writes an excellent account of polio and other great medical discoveries and advances of the past one hundred years.

Greer Williams, *Virus Hunters*. New York: Knopf, 1959. This books contains fascinating stories of the men and women involved in solving some of the most difficult viral diseases of the nineteenth and twentieth centuries. Salk's work is prominently and accurately described from a scientific perspective.

Works Consulted

Books

Richard Carter, *Breakthrough: The Saga of Jonas Salk.* New York: Trident Press, 1966. This book is considered the most authoritative biography of Jonas Salk. It primarily covers all of the events of Salk's life through the discovery of the polio vaccine. Because it was written in 1966, it does not touch on much of Salk's life at the Salk Institute.

Paul Heyer, *American Architecture: Ideas and Ideologies in the Late Twentieth Century.* Summerset, NJ: John Wiley & Sons, 1997. This book addresses a large number of innovative architectural designs, one of which is the Salk Institute.

John Rodman Paul, *A History of Poliomyelitis.* New Haven: Yale University Press, 1971. This scholarly work, written by a physician who took part in the search for a polio cure, documents polio research during the decades of 1950 and 1960. Paul presents an in-depth analysis of all of the steps leading to the final vaccines developed by Salk and Sabin.

Nina Gilden Seavey, Jane S. Smith, and Paul Wagner, *A Paralyzing Fear: The Triumph over Polio in America.* New York: TV Books, 1998. This book documents the history of polio in America. Its strength is its series of interviews with people who have been either victims of the virus, polio researchers, or doctors treating the disease. The book also contains an excellent selection of photographs.

Jane Smith, *Patenting the Sun: Polio and the Salk Vaccine.* New York: William Morrow, 1990. This book focuses on the experiences of children who suffered the effects of polio. It also discusses Jonas Salk's work creating the polio vaccine and many of the political and economic forces that impacted Salk and his friends and enemies. This book is oriented more toward adult than to adolescent readers.

Periodicals

Gilbert Cant, "Magnifying the Poliovirus," *Time,* November 16, 1953.

Marilyn Chase, "AIDS Scientist's Self-Inoculation Sparks Debate," *Wall Street Journal,* March 19, 1987.

Huntly Collins, "The Not-So-Glamourous Life of a Poster Child," *Philadelphia Inquirer,* February 23, 1999.

Anthony Fauci, "Still in the Trenches: Jonas Salk," *U.S. News & World Report,* July 9, 1990.

June Krieger, "What Price Fame to Dr. Salk," *New York Times Magazine,* July 17, 1955.

Neal Nathanson and Alexander Langmuir, "The Cutter Incident: Part I,"

American Journal of Hygiene, vol. 78, July 1963.

J.M. Oliver and B. Aylward, "Poliovirus Vaccine: Commentary," *Bulletin of the World Health Organization,* February 1999.

Science Digest, "The Creative Mind: Jonas Salk," June 1985.

Peter Stoler, "A Conversation with Jonas Salk," *Psychology Today,* March 1983.

Radio

"Profile of Man in an Iron Lung," *All Things Considered,* National Public Radio, August 21, 1994.

Websites

The American Gallery of Achievement (www.achievement.org/autodoc/page gen/lbmainmenu.html). This website focuses on American individuals who have shaped the twentieth century by their accomplishments. Each biographical sketch includes an interview as well as discussions about the person's achievements.

NBCI (http://nbci.msnbc.com/nbci.asp). The National Broadcasting Corporation's (NBC) official website contains hundreds of links to news and programming carried by NBC.

Index

research methods,
43–45, 47
Rivers, Thomas, 55,
56, 68
Robbins, Fred, 51
Roosevelt, Franklin
D., 22, 23, 48
Russian immigrants,
15–16

Sabin, Albert, 44, 52,
53, 56, 65
Salk, Donna (wife),
24–25, 42, 90
Salk, Dora (mother),
15–18
Salk, Jonas
AIDS research by,
92–95
awareness of polio
victims suffering
by, 61
criticism of, 47, 78,
79, 81–83, 96
curiosity of, 17–18
death of, 95–96
early life, 15–19
education of
college career,
19–21
medical internship,
26–28, 30
medical school,
23–25

by mother, 16–18
at Townsend
Harris High
School, 18–19
fame of, 65–67,
74–79, 81–83
favorite sayings of,
82
honors received by,
75–76
influenza vaccine
work of, 30–32, 34
marriages of, 24–25,
90
mother's influence
on, 15–18
move to University
of Pittsburgh by,
36–38
during 1980s, 92
philosophical ideas
of, 90–92, 97
as research assistant
to Thomas
Francis, 30–32,
34–35
research methods
of, 43–45, 47
Salk Institute
building of, 86–88
community of
scholars at, 88–89
funding for, 86
idea for, 85–86
Salk retires from, 92

Shannon, James,
78–79
Smith, Jane, 27–28,
47
Snow, C.P., 88
streptococcus
bacteria, 23
*Survival of the Wisest,
The*, 91–92
Szilard, Leo, 85, 88

T-cells, 94–95
Townsend Harris
High School, 18–19

University of
Michigan, 30–32,
34–35
University of
Pittsburgh Medical
School
opportunity at,
36–38
Salk leaves, 85–86

vaccines
adjuvants in, 56, 58
conventional
theories on, 28,
30
formalin formula
and, 52, 54

HIV, 92–95
immune system
  and, 29
live vs. dead viruses
  in, 28, 30, 34, 52, 68
potency of, 38
production of large
  quantities of,
  67–68
see also individual
  vaccines

viruses
  formalin inactivation
    of, 52, 54
  live vs. dead, in
    vaccines, 28, 30,
    34, 52, 68
  nature of, 33

Watson Home, 59–60,
  62–63

Weaver, Harry M., 38,
  40, 41
Weller, Thomas, 51
World Population and
  Human Values, 92
World War II, 30
Wright, Jessie, 59,
  60

Zwerlding, Daniel, 24

Picture Credits

Cover: Associated Press

© Bettmann/CORBIS, 13, 17, 20, 27, 32, 39, 43, 63, 64, 70, 73, 77, 83,

© CORBIS, 15, 22

© Digital Stock, 31

© Hulton-Archive by Getty Images, 37, 41, 49, 51, 54, 55, 60, 61, 66, 67, 75, 80, 81, 85, 88, 90, 93, 97

Library of Congress, 45

Martha Schierholz, 29

National Archives, 14, 19, 44, 53

© NIBSC/Science Source/Photo Researchers, Inc. 33, 40, 94

© OMIKRON/Science Source/Photo Researchers, Inc., 69

© Peter Aprahamian/CORBIS, 87

About the Author

James Barter received his undergraduate degree in history and classics at the University of California at Berkeley. This was followed by graduate studies in ancient history and archaeology at the University of Pennsylvania. Mr. Barter has taught history as well as Latin and Greek.

A Fulbright scholar at the American Academy in Rome, Mr. Barter has worked on archaeological sites in and around the city as well as on sites in the Naples area. Mr. Barter also has worked and traveled extensively in Greece.

Mr. Barter currently lives in Rancho Santa Fe, California, with his sixteen-year-old daughter Kalista, who is a student at Torrey Pines High School and works as a soccer referee. Mr. Barter's older daughter, Tiffany, also lives in Rancho Santa Fe, where she teaches violin and has a business arranging live music performances.